Physical Characteristics of the Sealyham Terrier

(from The Kennel Club breed standard)

Tail: Set in line with back and carried erect. Quarters should protrude beyond set of tail. Customarily docked.

Body: Medium in length, level and flexible with ribs well sprung. Chest broad and deep, well let down between forelegs.

Hindquarters: Notably powerful for size of dog. Thighs deep and muscular with well bent stifle. Hocks strong, well bent and parallel to each other.

Colour: All white or white with lemon, brown, blue or badger pied markings on head and ears.

Size: Height should not exceed 31 cms (12 ins) at shoulder. Ideal weight: dogs approx 9 kgs (20 lbs); bitches approx 8 kgs (18 lbs).

Feet: Round and cat-like with thick pads. Feet pointing directly forward.

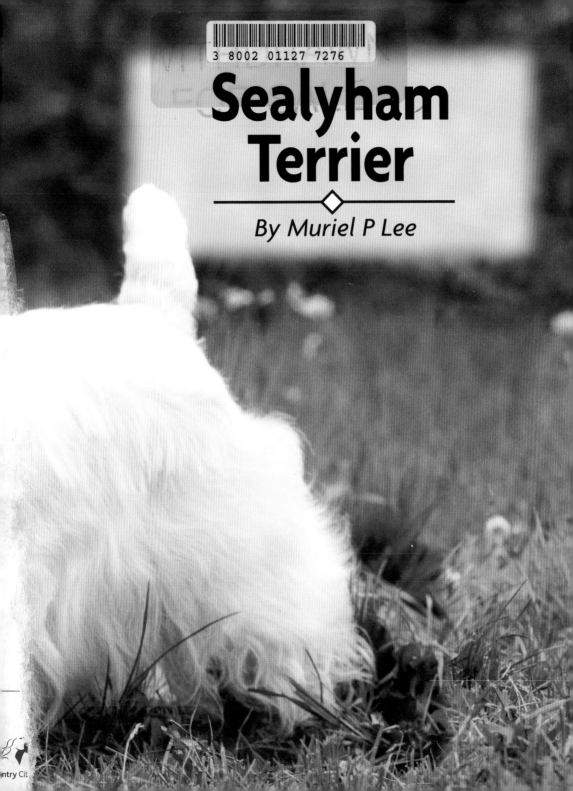

Sealyham Terrier

By Muriel P Lee

Contents

Copyright © 2004
Kennel Club Books, Inc.
Cover Design Patent: US 6,435,559 B2
Printed in South Korea

PUBLISHED IN THE UNITED KINGDOM BY:

INTERPET
PUBLISHING

Vincent Lane, Dorking, Surrey RH4 3YX England

ISBN 1-84286-060-7

Photography by Carol Ann Johnson and Michael Trafford with additional photographs by:

Norvia Behling, TJ Calhoun, Carolina Biological Supply, Doskocil, Isabelle Français, James Hayden-Yoav, James R Hayden, RBP, Bill Jonas, Dwight R Kuhn, Dr Dennis Kunkel, Mikki Pet Products, Phototake, Jean Claude Revy, Dr Andrew Spielman and Alice van Kempen.

Illustrations by Patricia Peters.

The publisher wishes to thank all of the owners of the dogs featured in this book, including Biddy & Harry Horn and Brenda Jones.

Having originated in the British Isles, the Sealyham Terrier was bred from existing terriers specifically to go after badgers, which often can be larger than a fully-grown Sealyham.

ORIGINS OF THE BREED

The history of the Sealyham Terrier traces back to 1850, making it a fairly old terrier breed. The Sealyham owes its being to breed inventor Captain John Edwardes, an active, rather eccentric sportsman, who lived in Havorfordwest, in the South of Wales near Fishguard.

Most of the dogs in the Terrier Group originated in the British Isles, with a few exceptions. The terrier name comes from the Latin word *terra*, meaning 'earth.' The terrier is a dog that has been bred to work beneath the ground to drive out small and large rodents, foxes and other animals that can be a nuisance to country life. They are intelligent, bright dogs with a very sturdy constitution. The Sealyham was bred specifically to go after the badger, an animal that can be larger in size than the Sealyham Terrier himself!

Captain Edwardes did not keep records of his breeding programme, but it is thought that the Welsh Corgi and the Dandie Dinmont Terrier, both breeds common in Wales, were in the background of his breedings. In addition, the now-extinct

Capt. Edwardes of Sealyham, the originator of the Sealyham breed, is unique in dogdom as being the only known sole creator of a major breed of dog. How he created this marvellous breed is not precisely known, as the Captain seems to have taken this secret with him to his grave.

Eventually, Captain Edwardes bred a dog that had a maximum of courage, was small enough to go to ground and could run all day with the horses and hounds.

At one time, Captain Edwardes had 16 packs of hounds with which the terriers ran, and each pack contained up to 30 well-mannered and well-managed dogs. Upon the captain's death in 1891, his daughter took over the Sealyham house and kennels. She remained a strong supporter of the Sealyham Terrier until the late 1930s.

THE BREED'S EARLY DAYS IN BRITAIN

In the early 1900s, the Sealyham was still a rather ragged-looking breed, some with long legs, others with thick skulls and others with silky rather than harsh coats. The breed was first shown in 1903 at a show in Havorfordwest, and it was noted that the judge had some difficulty in sorting out the entry because of the variations between the dogs. However, by 1908, Mr

Duck from the 1800s was the dam of the famous Ivo Challenger. She did not typify any specific breed of terrier, though she did possess similar coloration to the Sealyham.

Cheshire Terrier, possibly the Fox Terrier and the West Highland White Terrier was also crossed. Although it appears that a number of breeds were used to make up the Sealyham, the Captain chose the breeds carefully, always searching for the perfect dog. The Corgi and the Dandie Dinmont were used to shorten the legs, the latter incorporated to reinforce the terrier spirit; the Westie was introduced to reduce the size and to lend its pure white coloration; and the Cheshire Terrier added gameness and a stronger jaw.

Fred Lewis, a friend of Captain Edwardes, started seriously breeding Sealyhams under the Bach Kennel prefix and, within a few years, had bred some animals that he thought looked smart enough to be entered in a show. In 1910, he took some of his dogs to the famed Crystal Palace show in London, where the breed caused immediate interest as it had not been seen by the British dog-show folk prior to this time.

However, even by 1914, an entry of over 600 Sealys at the Pembrokeshire Hunt Club's show gave the judge a day's work because of the diversity in type. First prize went to Ivo Challenger, by Brass Bach and out of Duck. Mr Lewis noted that the merit of the winner came from the sire's side (out of his Bach breeding) as Duck 'bore not the slightest resemblance to any known terrier!'

When World War I broke out, breeding of dogs basically stopped

The prototypical terrier, the Fox Terrier, was used in the development of a number of other terrier breeds, among which is likely the Sealyham.

The Welsh Corgi was likely used to reduce the length of the Sealyham's legs. Shown here is a Cardigan Welsh Corgi.

A fellow short-legged terrier, the Dandie Dinmont is more ancient than the Sealyham and is credited by historians as one of the breed's likely progenitors.

in the UK and this was no exception with the Sealyham Terrier. However, by 1920 or so, the breeding and exhibiting of all breeds resumed.

During the 1920s and 1930s, the Brash Kennels of Mr R S de Quincey made up 17 champions, of which several were exported to the United States, where they not only continued their winning ways but also became top producers. Ch Brash Beau, sire of four champions, was said to be small but of superb type and quality. Ch Brash Beau Nash sired six champions, and Mr de Quincey thought that Beau was the best Sealyham of all time.

Sir Jocelyn Lucas, a dapper-looking Welsh gentleman and an avid sportsman, would keep up to

Noted for its solid white coat and smallish size, the West Highland White is speculated by cynologists as one of the contributing breeds to the Sealyham's creation.

200 Sealyhams in his Ilmer Kennels at one time, selling dogs to film stars as well as royalty, including Princess Margaret. He was keen on the hunting of badger, a tenacious furry animal with a tough hide and weighing up to 16 kgs (35 lbs). He bred dogs from 1920 to the 1950s, and only during World War II was his kennel reduced to 12 or so dogs. He was the author of an early book on the breed, *The New Book of the Sealyham Terrier*, printed in 1929. This book, although now rare, contains wonderful photos of Sealyhams' drawing badgers out of their dens.

By far, the most influential Sealyham Terrier kennel on either side of the Atlantic was the St Margaret Kennels of Mrs Cora Charters from Windsor. Her breeding programme, which expanded from 1920 to the 1950s, produced top winners and producers during every decade of its operation. She bred for dogs that were small and heavily boned. She bred many memorable Sealyhams, but the most well known were: Ch St Margaret Serene, sire of 8 champions; Ch St Margaret Snowman, sire of 7 champions; Ch St Margaret Magnificent of Clairedale, sire of 2 English and 16 American champions; Ch St Margaret Superlative of Robin Hill, sire of 9 American champions; and Ch St Margaret Swell Fella, sire of 2 English and 5 American

THE WHITE HUNTER'S COAT

A white dog was desired by many sportsmen, as the dog could not be easily confused with either a fox or an otter, as on occasion the Cairn Terrier had been. This confusion could lead to the dreadful mistake of the hunter's mistaking the dog for the prey and killing it.

champions. All of her great dogs made a positive impact upon the breed, which is still felt on both sides of the Atlantic.

THE SEALY GOES TO THE STATES

The Sealyham Terrier was exported to the United States in 1911 and received American Kennel Club (AKC) recognition in the same year. The American Sealyham Terrier Club was

THE SEALYHAM ACTIVITY CENTRE

Eventually the estate and lands of Captain John Edwardes were purchased by a consortium and turned into an activity centre offering accommodation, summer camping and a wealth of sports activities for children. In the spring of 2000, the Sealyham Terrier Club of England held its millennium show at this historic site, the birthplace of the breed.

Bred in 1933 by Capt R S de Quincey, Ch Brash Beacon follows the direct lineage of the original dogs bred by Capt. Edwardes.

founded in 1913. By 1917, the New York show had an entry of 46, compared to the 1912 show in which the entry was 5. After that, the breed gained immediate popularity and there was always a demand for puppies.

Impressive English imports found their way to the US. Delf Discriminate, from the Delf Kennels in Surrey, was exported and became an all-breed Best in Show winner and the sire of ten US champions. Another very active early American kennel was Mr and Mrs Russell Alger's Rensal Kennels, importing several winning English Sealys, including

One of the earliest shows organised for the breed in England, this informal show was chaired by Capt. Jack Howell in May 1914.

Ch Scotia Stylist, a great winning Sealyham from proven stock, was born in September 1927 and is a typical champion of that time.

Eng and Am Ch Brash Beau Ideal, in the late 1930s, who sired six English and eight American champions.

The Hemlock Hill Kennels of Mr and Mrs Alfred Geiger, Jr produced their homebred Ch Ivo Clyde, who became the first American-bred bitch to gain a championship. The Barberryhill Kennels, owned by Bayard Warren, bred Sealys for nearly three decades, from the 1920s to the 1940s. Mr Warren, a well-respected breeder and AKC judge, presided over some of America's more prestigious shows. Miss Helen Schweinler of the Croglin Kennels received her first Sealy in the 1920s and bred dogs through the mid-1950s. The kennel housed as many as 60 Sealys on occasion and, in 1938, there were 16 champions housed in the kennel. Ch Nutfield Silhouette, sired by Ch St Margaret Snowman, was shipped to the well-known Croglin Kennels. Ch Croglin Commando sired 15 champions and Ch Brash Best Man of Croglin sired 8 champions.

Ch Gunside Babs of Hollybourne, bred by Col. and Mrs A F Nicholson, was exported from Britain to the US and went Best in Show at the very prestigious Morris and Essex show in 1934. Again, with the onset of

World War II, breeding and dog shows in both America and the UK were greatly curtailed.

The next large and very influential kennel in the US, established by 1940, was the Robin Hill Kennels of Mrs Robert Choate. Mrs Choate not only bred top-winning and top-producing dogs but also imported the best dogs from England. The kennels were managed by Joe Thompson, but Mrs Choate made the rounds of the kennels every morning, looking over the dogs. She played an active role in the breedings, always looking for dogs that excelled in conformation and that retained the working terrier spirit. Robin Hill was active through the 1960s, producing 183 litters, with 33 champion bitches' producing

The famous Gunside Kennels, one of the early prominent kennels in the UK, is represented here by five generations of Gunsides breeding in the 1930s.

Ch Samphire Specialist, bred by Miss D Boydell Gibson, was born in August 1929.

63 champions and 18 dogs' siring about 100 champions.

Mrs W E Josten and her Hampton Hill Kennels joined the Sealyham ranks in the 1940s and 1950s, breeding good dogs as well as importing winning animals from Wales and England. Ch Hampton Hill Defiant sired 17 champion offspring, and Hampton Hill Hornet produced six champions. Ch Gunside Seapilot of Leckington was imported and sired five American champions. Hampton Hill provided the foundations for several American kennels.

In addition to those of Mrs Choate and Mrs Josten, other American kennels of note during the 1940s and 1950s were the Van Winkle Kennels of Mr and Mrs E Pennington Meyer, with over 30 champions carrying their prefix, and the Etherden Kennels of Sidney and Florence Etherden, which had top winners, among which there were approximately 40 champions. The Etherdens

Ch Hillsome Solo Flight, bred by Mrs A E Lifsham, was born in 1933.

were also principals in the founding of the Sealyham Terrier Club of Southern California, a club which has done much to promote the Sealyham on America's West Coast.

In the 1960s and 1970s, Mrs William Wimer and her Pool Forge Kennels bred outstanding Sealys in addition to importing some great English stock. Of special note were Eng and Am Ch St Margaret's Steven, group winner at America's foremost conformation show, the Westminster Kennel Club show; Eng and Am Ch Alcide of Axe, an all-breed Best in Show winner, group winner at Westminster and sire of eight champions; and Ch Hummerskott Harum Scarum, Best in Show winner and number-one Sealy in 1965. By far the biggest winner from this kennel was Eng and Am Ch Dersade Bobby's Girl. About 50 Sealys with the Pool Forge prefix became champions.

Nearly two dozen bitches from the Nutfield kennels of Col. and Mrs A F Nicholson.

William and Shirley Hitt of Sherwood Kennels and A William and Dolores Burdick of Dannyquest Kennels bred and showed Sealys in the 1960s. Dogs from both kennels were heavily line-bred on Eng and Am Ch Alcide of Axe. A top dog from the Dannyquest Kennel was Ch Vandon Village Vagrant, bred by Mrs H N Bilney in England and imported by the Burdicks. He produced 18 champion offspring, including 2 that were themselves top producers—Ch Pool Forge King's Ransom and Ch Sherwood Hill Magic Made, both of which sired 10 champions.

WHAT THE BADGER DOESN'T KNOW...

Sir Jocelyn Lucas wrote in his book: 'A badger dog is not meant to fight until the end of the day. His job is first to find if the badger is at home, and then locate him. Sometimes the badger doesn't wait to be located but charges the intruder anyway. A headstrong dog would fight and get chewed up. A good badger dog does not. He faces his enemy, but retires discreetly when the badger charges; but once the quarry is found he never ceases to throw his tongue. This has the dual effect of letting the diggers know where he is, and at the same time, to a certain extent, of stopping the badger, who presumably has not heard that barking dogs don't bite.'

BIS IN THE US

In the US, the Sealyham Terrier has won both of the country's most prestigious shows, the all-terrier show at Montgomery County and the all-breed show in New York City, the Westminster Kennel Club. Here are the victors of those shows over the years:

BEST IN SHOW AT MONTGOMERY COUNTY KENNEL CLUB:
1936 Ch Wolvey Norl of Clairedale
1979 Ch Goodspsice Tarragon
1995 Ch Fanfare's Goodfellow

BEST IN SHOW AT WESTMINSTER KENNEL CLUB:
1924 Ch Barberryhill Bootlegger
1927 Ch Pinegrade Perfection
1936 Ch St Margaret Magnificent of
      Claredale
1977 Ch Dersade Bobby's Girl

One of the longest-lasting kennels in the US was the Rinklestone Kennels of M Thelma Miller. She was active in the breed for over five decades, from the 1930s to the 1980s. At least 75 champions came from her kennel, all owner-conditioned and owner-handled. She was also active in obedience, placing obedience degrees on six of her brood bitches. She was an AKC judge of Sealyham and Scottish Terriers in addition to being an approved obedience judge. She was the true fancier and breeder, giving her

Ch St Margaret Merit was portrayed in wool! He was an invaluable stud dog during the 1930s, continuing the original famous line of Brash Sealyhams.

time and energies to the breed that she so dearly loved.

Mrs Richard Wood III (Patsy) of the Penllyn prefix has been a strong Sealy supporter for over 40 years. Ch Penllyn Paprika of Goodspice is the top-producing bitch in the breed with 13 champions. Patsy bred the first American champion to be sent to England, where he became an English champion, Am and Eng Ch Penllyn Proper Bloke II. He went to David Winsley and Kevin Holmes and became the top Sealy in England in 1993. One can see that the English dogs continued to make an impact throughout the 20th century on dogs on both sides of the pond.

MONTGOMERY COUNTY: AN AMERICAN TERRIER TRADITION

Montgomery County Kennel Club is the premier all-terrier show in the United States. Nearly all of the terrier breeds hold their national specialities at this show, which is held on the first weekend in October in Ambler, Pennsylvania. The top terriers from throughout the country are exhibited and spectators come from around the world to see over 2500 exhibits, representing all of the terrier breeds.

MEMORIES OF AN EARLY SEALY KENNEL

Phoebe Cuming wrote about her aunt's kennel in the 1920s: 'At the age of 14 I started work at my aunt's kennel where there were 60 dogs. The wooden floors had to be scrubbed every day. Straw bedding was used in winter with sawdust of the floors and this had to be burnt daily. I was left to manage the kennels on my own as my aunt did no kennel work and only came out to criticise, very severely. The dogs were fed on biscuit meal soaked in broth from bullocks' heads, which I loathed cooking because of the eyes. I had three trimming tools, a brush, a comb and my fingers.'

WORLD-WIDE IMPACT OF THE BRITISH SEALY

The last three decades of the 20th century saw a number of English breeders' breeding top-notch animals that have had impact around the world. Pat Crick of Shenden Kennels bred a number of champions but of note was Ch Posh Etherden, sire of five champions. Overall, 10 Shenden males sired 17 English and American champions, and 14 bitches produced 24 English and American champions.

The Polrose Kennels of Mrs Phoebe Cuming was another kennel that produced a number of winning dogs. Ch Polrose Pace Setter, exported to America, sired eight champions and, overall, 17 Polrose dogs produced and sired 34 English and American champions.

Derek Thomas, a popular Welshman, of Dersade Kennels, judged the Montgomery County Kennel Club Show in the US in 1999, this being the most prestigious all-terrier show in America.

By far his biggest winner was Eng and Am Ch Dersade Bobby's Girl, 'Binny,' exported to Mrs William Wimer and handled expertly by Peter Green. She had a remarkable show career, finishing her American championship in three consecutive shows over the 1973 Montgomery County weekend. In 1974, she won the Quaker Oats award with 42 Bests in Show and 74 group firsts, including Best of Breed at Montgomery County and a group fourth placement. In 1975, she was again Best of Breed at Montgomery County and received a group second placement. She reached the peak of the dog world when she was Best in Show at the Westminster Kennel Club in 1977.

Mrs B A Horne of Topstage Kennels bred several top producers: Ch Topstage Canada Dry sired four champions and Eng and Am Ch Topstage Raffles, exported to Sarah Sweatt in the US, was the sire of six champions.

Mrs Stella Rootes of Torset Kennels certainly made an impact

The Sealyham
Terrier today
competes at
shows world-wide
and has won many
top awards at
major conforma-
tion shows in the
UK and US.

BRAIN AND BRAWN

Since dogs have been inbred for centuries, their physical and mental characteristics are constantly being changed to suit man's desires for hunting, retrieving, scenting, guarding and warming their masters' laps. During the past 150 years, dogs have been judged according to physical characteristics as well as functional abilities. Few breeds can boast a genuine balance between physique, working ability and temperament.

on the breed in America when she exported Ch Torset Touch of Class to Margery Goode in the US. By the turn of the 21st century, he had sired about 40 champions, making him the all-time leading sire of Sealy champions in the world.

CANADA AND BEYOND

In Canada, several Sealy kennels have been well known for years. In 1978, Kay and Lou Guimond, of the Wirehill Fox Terrier Kennels, acquired Am Eng Can Ch Roderick of Jenmist for their stud force after he was retired from his show career. Imported from England and handled by George Ward, 'Roddy' made up his American championship with three Bests in Show from the classes! He was shown in Canada on a limited basis, where he won several group firsts in

addition to Best in Show at the Sportsmen's Show. When he retired, he had 22 all-breed Bests in Show. In addition, he had also been a top Sealyham in the UK for his breeder, Mr Somerfield. The Wirehill Kennels has produced winners throughout North America.

The Abricot Kennels, owned and operated by Bill and Madeleine Greenwood, bred Am Eng Can Ch Abricot Blenheim Bloke, the top-winning Canadian Sealy of all time. A multiple Best in Show winner, he was exported to Topstage Kennels in England, where he won 10 Challenge Certificates and many all-breed Bests in Show. His offspring can be found throughout North America, England and the Continent.

The Sealyham Terrier is a popular breed in the Scandinavian countries, where many good representatives of the breed have been produced. The Silver Moon Kennel of Majvi and Mats Niveborn in Sweden owned Int and Nord Ch Jackass Jack, a top-winning Swedish Sealy with 75 Bests of Breed and 40 group placements.

There are Sealys throughout Europe, in New Zealand and in South America. Indeed, one would think that Captain Edwardes would be very pleased to see how far his tough little dog has gone in the world!

Characteristics of the
SEALYHAM TERRIER

ARE YOU READY FOR A SEALY?

The Sealyham Terrier is a sturdy dog that projects an independent and sometimes stubborn attitude. He is a busy dog and he likes to be on his toes, watching for squirrels and rabbits, greeting his master and guarding his property. Whatever the job, he is quick and energetic. He's an appealing chum with a real personality who loves to be active and busy. The Sealyham Terrier is 'below the knee' in size but, in spite of his size, he is a masculine dog who does not show any sign of timidity or shyness. If you are looking for a sedentary lap dog, this will not be the breed for you.

This is an independent dog who, on frequent occasion, will want to do things his way. He requires a master who will have patience with him and who will not let him have the upper hand in the household. Obedience training, especially the basic commands, is beneficial for all dogs. Upon completion of the obedience course, you should have a dog that will come when called, sit when expected and walk next to you like a gentleman when taking his daily constitutional.

The Sealyham will adjust easily to children, but children must understand his independent nature, his need for space and his sense of dignity. This is not a dog to ride upon like a pony nor to drag around by his ears. This is a dignified dog who likes to join in the fun of the household but does not like to be mocked or teased.

This is a no-nonsense dog. The Sealy will not stand in the garden and bark for hours as some dogs will, but, if he hears a noise, he will alert his owner. He

MEET THE AWTA

The American Working Terrier Association (AWTA), founded in 1971, was formed to encourage and preserve the natural instinct of earth terriers. The dogs' instincts are tested, and they are to enter an underground tunnel and react in a positive manner when facing the quarry. A Working Certificate is issued to dogs that qualify for working in a natural den. The AWTC issues Working, Hunting and Gameness Certificates.

you have a good canine citizen that everyone will enjoy!

HEALTH CONCERNS

Sealyham Terriers, like all breeds, do have some health problems of which you should be aware. By and large, Sealyham Terriers are healthy dogs, as are most other terriers, but be certain to buy your puppy from a reputable breeder and ask the breeder if he has experienced any health problems in his line.

The following health concerns in the Sealyham involve eye problems, skin allergies and deafness. Let us look at each to understand the concerns more fully.

DEAFNESS

Deafness is primarily prominent in breeds with a white or merle coat. The ear canals open at about two weeks of age and deafness

The eyes and ears of the Sealyham are two most critical features pertaining to the breed's health. Be certain that your selected breeder has screened her stock for potential health problems.

will stand his ground but his actions are usually defensive, protecting his territory as a little soldier. However, if pushed into a fight, he will not back down.

Some basic rules of dog ownership and care will lead you and your Sealyham to a mutually rewarding life together. Always walk your Sealy on a leash or keep him in a securely fenced garden, and do not allow him to run loose through the neighbourhood. Do not allow him to bark for no reason, and keep him clean and groomed. You will find that

SKIN PROBLEMS

Eczema and dermatitis are skin problems that occur in many breeds and they can often be tricky problems to solve. Frequent bathing of the dog will remove skin oils and will cause the problem to worsen. Allergies to food or to something in the environment can also cause the problem. Consider trying homeopathic remedies in addition to seeing your vet for direction.

will not be noticed before this time. There are several tests, particularly behavioural tests, that can be given by the owner of a dog when it is suspected that there is an hearing problem. The hearing loss can be either unilateral or partial bilateral. Take your dog to a vet when you suspect that there is an hearing problem. Many university veterinary schools also do testing. There is no treatment for deafness, but many of these dogs can be wonderful pets when properly trained.

SKIN ALLERGIES

Skin allergies can occur in any breed but are more common in the light-coloured breeds. Your dog will itch, scratch or chew on an area, and hair loss will be noticeable as well as redness of the affected area. Try to determine what the dog is allergic to, such as grass, dirt, his bedding or possibly something in his diet. Take your dog to the vet and see what he feels to be the problem and what he suggests should be used for a cure. Skin problems can be difficult problems to clear up and do require patience on the owner's part.

EYE PROBLEMS

Potential eye problems in the Sealy consist of retinal dysplasia, lens luxation, cataracts and glaucoma. Retinal dysplasia is a

DOGS, DOGS, GOOD FOR YOUR HEART!

People usually purchase dogs for companionship, but studies show that dogs can help to improve their owners' health and level of activity, as well as lower a human's risk of coronary heart disease. Without even realising it, when a person puts time into exercising, grooming and feeding a dog, he also puts more time into his own personal health care. Dog owners establish more routine schedules for their dogs to follow, which can have positive effects on a human's health. Dogs also teach us patience, offer unconditional love and provide the joy of having a furry friend to pet!

congenital disorder with abnormal development of the retina. This is an inheritable problem caused by a simple recessive gene. Reputable breeders will test their dogs to make certain that they are not carriers of this gene. Lens luxation is the rupture of the zonular attachments between the lens and ciliary body. Trauma, inheritance, glaucoma, inflammation and ageing all can contribute to the change in lens position. Again, this is a congenital problem, but the condition usually can be treated with medications.

ELIMINATING PROBLEMS

Many breed clubs in both Britain and America are working to eradicate the congenital problems within their breeds; the national kennel clubs support health-related research as well. The Kennel Club's Charitable Trust supports the study of canine diseases, and the UK's Animal Health Trust works to fight disease and eliminate inherited problems. In the US, the AKC's Canine Health Foundation has been very active in searching for the sources of various congenital problems.

Breed Standard for the
SEALYHAM TERRIER

As breeders started exhibiting at dog shows, it was realised that there must be more uniformity within the breed, i.e. all puppies in a litter should look alike as well as being of the same type as their sire and dam. Each breed recognised by The Kennel Club has a standard, a written description of the breed, that gives the reader a mental picture of what the specific breed should look like. All reputable breeders strive to produce animals that will meet the requirements of the standard.

Many breeds were developed for specific purposes, such as hunting, retrieving, going to ground, coursing, guarding or herding. The terriers were all bred to go to ground and to pursue vermin; the Sealyham was bred specifically to go after badgers. In addition to having dogs that look like proper Sealyham Terriers, the standard assures that members of the breed will have the personality, disposition and intelligence that are sought after. Standards were originally written by fanciers who had a love and a concern for the breed. They knew that the essential characteristics of the breed were unlike any other breed and that care must be taken that these characteristics were maintained through the generations.

As time progressed and breeders became more aware that certain parts of the dog needed a better description or more definition, breeders would meet together and work out a new standard. However, standards for any breed are never changed on a whim, and serious study and

BREEDER'S BLUEPRINT

If you are considering breeding your bitch, it is very important that you are familiar with the breed standard. Reputable breeders breed with the intention of producing dogs that are as close as possible to the standard and that contribute to the advancement of the breed. Study the standard for both physical appearance and temperament, and make certain your bitch and your chosen stud dog measure up.

Profile of a dog
of correct type,
balance and
proportion.

exchange between breeders take place before any move is made. In Britain, The Kennel Club has final say on any and all alterations to the breed standards.

THE KENNEL CLUB STANDARD FOR THE SEALYHAM TERRIER

General Appearance: Free-moving, active, balanced and of great substance in small compass. General outline oblong, not square.

Characteristics: Sturdy, game and workmanlike.

Temperament: Alert and fearless but of friendly disposition.

Head and Skull: Skull slightly domed and wide between ears. Cheek bones not prominent. Punishing square jaw, powerful and long. Nose black.

Eyes: Dark, well set, round, of medium size. Dark, pigmented eye rims preferred but unpigmented tolerated.

Ears: Medium-sized, slightly rounded at tip and carried at side of cheek.

Mouth: Teeth level and strong with canines fitting well into each other and long for size of dog. Jaws strong with regular scissor bite, i.e. upper teeth closely overlapping lower teeth and set square to the jaws.

Neck: Fairly long, thick and muscular on well laid shoulders.

Forequarters: Forelegs short, strong and as straight as possible consistent with chest being well let down. Point of shoulder in line with point of elbow which should be close to side of chest.

Body: Medium in length, level and flexible with ribs well sprung. Chest broad and deep, well let down between forelegs.

Hindquarters: Notably powerful for size of dog. Thighs deep and muscular with well bent stifle. Hocks strong, well bent and parallel to each other.

Feet: Round and cat-like with thick pads. Feet pointing directly forward.

Tail: Set in line with back and carried erect. Quarters should protrude beyond set of tail. Customarily docked.

Gait/Movement: Brisk and vigorous with plenty of drive.

THE IDEAL SPECIMEN

According to The Kennel Club, 'The Breed Standard is the "Blueprint" of the ideal specimen in each breed approved by a governing body, e.g. The Kennel Club, the Fédération Cynologique Internationale (FCI) and the American Kennel Club.'

'The Kennel Club writes and revises Breed Standards taking account of the advice of Breed Councils/Clubs. Breed Standards are not changed lightly to avoid "changing the standard to fit the current dogs" and the health and well-being of future dogs is always taken into account when new standards are prepared or existing ones altered.'

**Head study
showing correct
balance and type.**

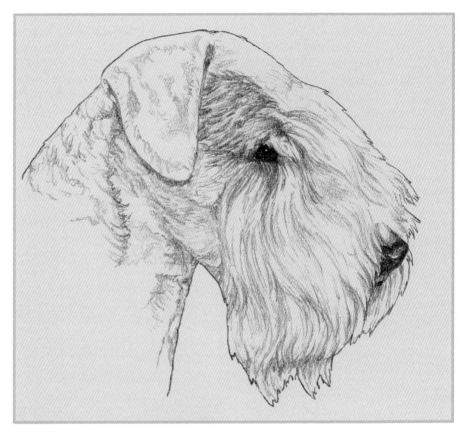

**The skull should
be slightly domed
and wide
between the ears.**

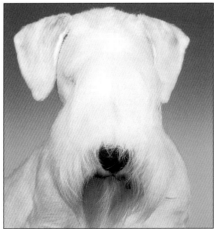

Coat: Long, hard and wiry top coat with weather-resistant undercoat.

Colour: All white or white with lemon, brown, blue or badger pied markings on head and ears. Much black and heavy ticking undesirable.

Size: Height should not exceed 31 cms (12 ins) at shoulder. Ideal weight: dogs approx 9 kgs (20 lbs); bitches approx 8 kgs (18 lbs).

BREEDING CONSIDERATIONS

The decision to breed your dog is one that must be considered carefully and researched thoroughly before moving into action. Some people believe that breeding will make their bitches happier or that it is an easy way to make money. Unfortunately, indiscriminate breeding only worsens the rampant problem of pet overpopulation, as well as putting a considerable dent in your purse. As for the bitch, the entire process from mating through whelping is not an easy one and puts your pet under considerable stress. Last, but not least, consider whether or not you have the means to care for an entire litter of pups. Without a reputation in the field, your attempts to sell the pups may be unsuccessful.

General conformation, overall balance, type and substance are main criteria.

Faults: Any departure from the foregoing points should be considered a fault and the seriousness with which the fault should be regarded should be in exact proportion to its degree.

Note: Male animals should have two apparently normal testicles fully descended into the scrotum.

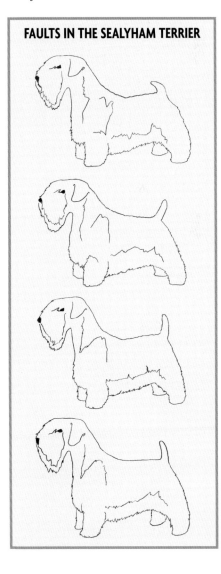

FAULTS IN THE SEALYHAM TERRIER

Long back, loaded upright shoulders, dip behind shoulders, gay tail.

Short, thick neck, upright loaded shoulders fall away to underdeveloped rear and 'two o'clock' tail.

Thin, underdeveloped neck, high in shoulders with dip behind them, high in rear with low tailset, straight behind, lacking angulation.

A bit long and too high on leg, straight front and rear, large ears.

FINDING THE IDEAL SEALY FOR YOU

If you are convinced that the Sealyham Terrier is the ideal dog for you, it's time to learn about where to find a puppy and what to look for. Although the Sealy isn't the most numerically strong of the terrier breeds, locating a litter of Sealyhams should not present a problem for the new owner. You should enquire about breeders who enjoy a good reputation in the breed. You are looking for an established breeder with outstanding dog ethics and a strong commitment to the breed. New owners should have as many questions as they have doubts. An established breeder is indeed the one to answer your four million questions and make you comfortable with your choice of the Sealy. An established breeder will sell you a puppy at a fair price if, and only if, the breeder determines that you are a suitable, worthy owner of his dogs. An established breeder can be relied upon for advice, no matter what time of day or night. A reputable breeder will accept a puppy back, without questions, should you decide that this is not the right dog for you.

Choosing a breeder is an important first step in dog ownership, and the breeder's reputation and commitment to the breed are more important than convenience of location or cost.

PUPPY APPEARANCE

Your puppy should have a well-fed appearance but not a distended abdomen, which may indicate worms or incorrect feeding, or both. The body should be firm, with a solid feel. The skin of the abdomen should be pale pink and clean, without signs of scratching or rash. Check the hind legs to make certain that dewclaws were removed, if any were present at birth.

Fortunately, the majority of Sealyham breeders is devoted to the breed and its well-being. New owners should have little problem finding a reputable breeder who doesn't live on the other side of the country. The Kennel Club is able to recommend breeders of healthy, sound Sealyham Terriers, as can any local all-breed club or Sealyham club.

Potential owners are encouraged to attend dog shows to see the Sealyham Terriers in action, to meet the owners and handlers firsthand and to get an idea of what Sealyhams look like outside a photographer's lens. Provided you approach the handlers when they are not terribly busy with the dogs, most are more than willing to answer questions, recommend breeders and give advice.

Once you have contacted and met a breeder or two and made your choice about which breeder is best suited to your needs, it's time to visit the litter. Keep in mind that many top breeders have waiting lists. Sometimes new owners have to wait as long as two years for a puppy. If you are really committed to the breeder whom you've selected, then you will wait (and hope for an early arrival!).

If you are choosing a Sealyham Terrier as a pet dog and not a show dog, you simply should select a pup that is friendly, attractive and healthy.

PUPPY SELECTION
Your selection of a good puppy can be determined by your needs. A show potential or a good pet? It is your choice. Every puppy, however, should be of good temperament. Although show-quality puppies are bred and raised with emphasis on physical conformation, responsible breeders strive for equally good temperament. Do not buy from a breeder who concentrates solely on physical beauty at the expense of personality.

Sealyham litters generally average four to five puppies, so selection will not be too overwhelming, compared to larger breeds that have litters of ten or more. The choice of male versus female is largely a matter of personal preference, though males tend to be slightly more aggressive than the females. Always check the bite of your selected puppy to be sure

Once you've decided that the Sealy is the breed for you, it is necessary to select a responsible breeder. You can recognise a dedicated breeder from the quality of her puppies and her genuine concern about their well-being.

that it is neither overshot nor undershot. This may not be too noticeable on a young puppy, but will become more evident as the puppy gets older.

Breeders commonly allow visitors to see their litters by around the fifth or sixth week, and puppies leave for their new homes between the eighth and tenth week. Breeders who permit their puppies to leave early are more interested in your pounds than in their puppies' well-being. Puppies need to learn the rules of the pack from their dams, and most dams continue teaching the pups manners and dos and don'ts until around the eighth week. Breeders spend significant amounts of time with the Sealyham toddlers so that the pups are able to interact with the 'other species,' i.e. humans. Given the long history that dogs and humans have, bonding between the two species is natural but must be nurtured. A well-bred, well-socialised Sealyham pup wants nothing more than to be near you and please you.

COMMITMENT OF OWNERSHIP

After considering all of these factors, you have most likely already made some very important decisions about selecting your puppy. You have chosen a Sealy, which means that you have decided which characteristics you want in a dog and which type of dog will best fit into your family and lifestyle. If you have selected a breeder, you have gone a step further—you have done your research and found a responsible, conscientious person who breeds quality Sealys and who should be a reliable source of help as you and your puppy adjust to life together. If you have observed a litter in action, you have obtained a firsthand look at the dynamics of a puppy 'pack' and, thus, you have learned about each pup's individual personality—perhaps you have even found one that particularly appeals to you.

However, even if you have not yet found the Sealyham puppy of your dreams, observing pups will help you learn to recognise certain behaviour and to determine what a pup's behaviour indicates about his temperament. You will be able to pick out which pups are the leaders, which ones are less outgoing, which ones are confident, which ones are shy, playful, friendly, aggressive, etc. Equally as important, you will learn to recognise what an healthy pup should look and act like. All of these things will help you in your search, and when you find the Sealyham Terrier that was meant for you, you will know it!

Researching your breed, selecting a responsible breeder and observing as many pups as possible are all important steps on the way to dog ownership. It may seem like a lot of effort...and you have not even taken the pup home yet! Remember, though, you cannot be too careful when it comes to deciding on the type of dog you want and finding out

TIME TO GO HOME

Breeders rarely release puppies until they are eight to ten weeks of age. This is an acceptable age for most breeds of dog, excepting toy breeds, which are not released until around 12 weeks, given their petite sizes. If a breeder has a puppy that is 12 weeks of age or older, it is likely well socialised and house-trained. Be sure that it is otherwise healthy before deciding to take it home.

DOCUMENTATION

Two important documents you will get from the breeder are the pup's pedigree and registration certificate. The breeder should register the litter and each pup with The Kennel Club, and it is necessary for you to have the paperwork if you plan on showing or breeding in the future.

Make sure you know the breeder's intentions on which type of registration he will obtain for the pup. There are limited registrations that may prohibit the dog from being shown, bred or competing in non-conformation trials such as Working or Agility if the breeder feels that the pup is not of sufficient quality to do so. There is also a type of registration that will permit the dog in non-conformation competition only.

On the reverse side of the registration certificate, the new owner can find the transfer section, which must be signed by the breeder.

about your prospective pup's background. Buying a puppy is not—or should not be—just another whimsical purchase. This is one instance in which you actually do get to choose your own family! You may be thinking that buying a puppy should be fun—it should not be so serious and so much work. Keep in mind that your puppy is not a cuddly stuffed toy or decorative lawn ornament; rather, he is a living creature that will become a real member of your family. You will come to realise that, while buying a puppy is a pleasurable and exciting endeavour, it is not something to be taken lightly. Relax…the fun will start when the pup comes home!

Always keep in mind that a puppy is nothing more than a baby in a furry disguise…a baby who is virtually helpless in a human world and who trusts his owner for fulfilment of his basic needs for survival. In addition to food, water and shelter, your pup needs care, protection, guidance and love. If you are not prepared to commit to this, then you are not prepared to own a dog.

Wait a minute, you say. How hard could this be? All of my neighbours own dogs and they

INSURANCE
Many good breeders will offer you insurance with your new puppy, which is an excellent idea. The first few weeks of insurance will probably be covered free of charge or with only minimal cost, allowing you to take up the policy when this expires. If you own a pet dog, it is sensible to take out such a policy as veterinary fees can be high, although routine vaccinations and boosters are not covered. Look carefully at the many insurance options open to you before deciding which suits you best.

ARE YOU A FIT OWNER?
If the breeder from whom you are buying a puppy asks you a lot of personal questions, do not be insulted. Such a breeder wants to be sure that you will be a fit provider for his puppy.

seem to be doing just fine. Why should I have to worry about all of this? Well, you should not worry about it; in fact, you will probably find that once your Sealyham pup gets used to his new home, he will fall into his place in the family quite naturally. However, it never hurts to emphasise the commitment of dog ownership. With some time

Provide your puppy with safe chew toys before he finds 'toys' of his own. Make the house rules clear to your Sealy puppy from the very first day.

When you bring your new puppy into your home, you are bringing him into what will become his home as well. Obviously, you did not buy a puppy with the intentions of catering to his every whim and allowing him to 'rule the roost,' but in order for a puppy to grow into a stable, well-adjusted dog, he has to feel comfortable in his surroundings. Remember, he is

and patience, it is really not too difficult to raise a curious and exuberant Sealyham pup to be a well-adjusted and well-mannered adult dog—a dog that could be your most loyal friend.

PREPARING PUPPY'S PLACE IN YOUR HOME

Researching your breed and finding a breeder are only two aspects of the 'homework' you will have to do before taking your Sealyham puppy home. You will also have to prepare your home and family for the new addition. Much as you would prepare a nursery for a newborn baby, you will need to designate a place in your home that will be the puppy's own. How you prepare your home will depend on how much freedom the dog will be allowed. Whatever you decide, you must ensure that he has a place that he can 'call his own.'

PREPARING FOR PUP

Unfortunately, when a puppy is bought by someone who does not take into consideration the time and attention that dog ownership requires, it is the puppy who suffers when he is either abandoned or placed in a shelter by a frustrated owner. So all of the 'homework' you do in preparation for your pup's arrival will benefit you both. The more informed you are, the more you will know what to expect and the better equipped you will be to handle the ups and downs of raising a puppy. Hopefully, everyone in the household is willing to do his part in raising and caring for the pup. The anticipation of owning a dog often brings a lot of promises from excited family members: 'I will walk him every day,' 'I will feed him,' 'I will house-train him,' etc., but these things take time and effort, and promises easily can be forgotten once the novelty of the new pet has worn off.

leaving the warmth and security of his mother and littermates, as well as the familiarity of the only place he has ever known, so it is important to make his transition as easy as possible. By preparing a place in your home for the puppy, you are making him feel as welcome as possible in a strange new place. It should not take him long to get used to it, but the sudden shock of being trans-planted is somewhat traumatic for a young pup. Imagine how a small child would feel in the same situation—that is how your puppy must be feeling. It is up to you to reassure him and to let him know, 'Little chap, you are going to like it here!'

WHAT YOU SHOULD BUY

CRATE
To someone unfamiliar with the use of crates in dog training, it may seem like punishment to shut a dog in a crate, but this is not the case at all. Although all breeders do not advocate crate training,

more and more breeders and trainers are recommending crates as preferred tools for show puppies as well as pet puppies.

Crates are not cruel—crates have many humane and highly effective uses in dog care and training. For example, crate training is a popular and remark-ably successful house-training method. In addition, a crate can keep your dog safe during travel and, perhaps most importantly, a crate provides your dog with a place of his own in your home. It serves as a 'doggie bedroom' of sorts—your Sealy can curl up in his crate when he wants to sleep

Signs of an healthy puppy include a moist nose, clear eyes, a pink tongue, a shiny coat and an happy tempera-ment.

PHOTO COURTESY OF DOSKOCIL.

two most popular types: wire or
fibreglass. There are advantages
and disadvantages to each type.
For example, a wire crate is more
open, allowing the air to flow
through and affording the dog a
view of what is going on around
him, while a fibreglass crate is
sturdier. Both can double as travel
crates, providing protection for
the dog. A small to medium-size
crate will be necessary for a fully-
grown Sealy, who stands approximately 31 cms (12 ins) at that
shoulder. Purchase a crate for
your Sealyham puppy that will

CRATE-TRAINING TIPS

During crate training, you should
partition off the section of the crate
in which the pup stays. If he is given
too big an area, this will hinder your
training efforts. Crate training is based
on the fact that a dog does not like
to soil his sleeping quarters, so it is
ineffective to keep a pup in a crate
that is so big that he can eliminate in
one end and get far enough away
from it to sleep. Also, you want to
make the crate den-like for the pup.
Blankets and a favourite toy will make
the crate cosy for the small pup; as he
grows, you may want to evict some of
his 'roommates' to make more room.

It will take some coaxing at first,
but be patient. Given some time to
get used to it, your pup will adapt
to his new home-within-an-home
quite nicely.

or when he just needs a break.
Many dogs sleep in their crates
overnight. With soft bedding and
his favourite toy, a crate becomes
a cosy pseudo-den for your dog.
Like his lupine ancestors, he too
will seek out the comfort and
retreat of a den, and the crate is a
bit more comfortable than an hole
in the ground.

As far as purchasing a crate,
the type that you buy is up to you.
It will most likely be one of the

These two toddlers are becoming acclimated to a travelling crate. Of course, for actual training purposes, each pup must have a crate of his own.

accommodate him as an adult, keeping in mind that the dog must be able to sit, stand and lie down comfortably.

BEDDING

Veterinary bedding in the dog's crate will help the dog feel more at home, and you may also like to pop in a small blanket. First, this will take the place of the leaves, twigs, etc., that the pup would use in the wild to make a den; the pup can make his own 'burrow' in the crate. Although your pup is far removed from his den-making ancestors, the denning instinct is still a part of his genetic makeup. Second, until you take your pup home, he has been sleeping amid the warmth of his mother and littermates, and while a blanket is not the same as a warm, breathing body, it still provides heat and something with which to snuggle. You will want to wash your pup's bedding frequently in case he has a toileting 'accident' in his crate, and replace or remove any blanket that becomes ragged and starts to fall apart.

TOYS

Toys are a must for dogs of all ages, especially for curious playful pups. Puppies are the 'children' of the dog world, and what child does not love toys? Chew toys provide enjoyment for both dog and owner—your dog will enjoy playing with his favourite toys, while you will enjoy the fact that they distract him from chewing on your expensive shoes and leather sofa. Puppies love to chew; in fact, chewing is a physical need for pups as they are teething, and everything looks appetising! The full range of your possessions— from old tea towel to Oriental carpet—are fair game in the eyes of a teething pup. Puppies are not all that discerning when it comes to finding something literally to 'sink their teeth into'—everything tastes great!

Sealyham puppies are fairly aggressive chewers and only the hardest, strongest toys should be offered to them. Sealys like rubber balls, but be sure they are hard and indestructible. Breeders advise owners to resist stuffed toys, because they can become de-stuffed in no time. The overly excited pup may ingest the stuffing, which is neither digestible nor nutritious.

Similarly, squeaky toys are quite popular, but must be avoided for the Sealyham. Perhaps a squeaky toy can be used as an aid in training, but not for free play. If a pup 'disembowels' one of these, the small plastic squeaker inside can be dangerous if swallowed. Monitor the condition of all your pup's toys carefully and get rid of any that have been chewed to the point of becoming potentially dangerous.

Be careful of natural bones, which have a tendency to splinter into sharp, dangerous pieces. Also be careful of rawhide, which can turn into pieces that are easy to swallow and become a mushy mess on your carpet.

LEAD

A nylon lead is probably the best option, as it is the most resistant to puppy teeth should your pup take a liking to chewing on his lead. Of course, this is an habit that should be nipped in the bud, but, if your pup likes to chew on his lead, he has a very slim chance of being able to chew through the strong nylon. Nylon leads are also lightweight, which is good for a young Sealyham who is just getting used to the idea of walking on a lead. For everyday walking and safety purposes, the nylon lead is a good choice.

As your pup grows up and gets used to walking on the lead, you may want to purchase a flexible lead. These leads allow you to extend the length to give the dog a broader area to explore or to shorten the length to keep the dog

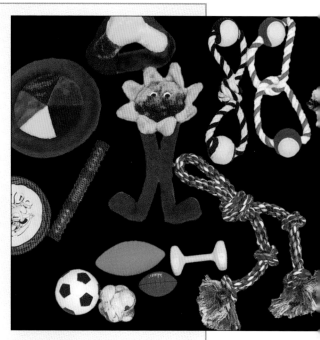

TOYS, TOYS, TOYS!

With a big variety of dog toys available, and so many that look like they would be a lot of fun for a dog, be careful in your selection. It is amazing what a set of puppy teeth can do to an innocent-looking toy, so, obviously, safety is a major consideration. Be sure to choose the most durable products that you can find. Hard nylon bones and toys are a safe bet, and many of them are offered in different scents and flavours that will be sure to capture your dog's attention. It is always fun to play a game of catch with your dog, and there are balls and flying discs that are specially made to withstand dog teeth.

Your local pet
shop will have an
array of dog leads
from which you
can make a
selection for
your Sealy.

near you. Of course, there are leads designed for training purposes and specially made leather harnesses, but these are not necessary for routine walks.

COLLAR

Your pup should get used to wearing a collar all the time since you will want to attach his ID tags to it; plus, you have to attach the lead to something! A lightweight nylon collar is a good choice. Make certain that the collar fits snugly enough so that the pup cannot wriggle out of it, but is loose enough so that it will not be uncomfortably tight around the pup's neck. You should be able to fit a finger between the pup's neck and the collar. It may take some time for your pup to get used to wearing the collar, but soon he will not even notice that it is there. Choke collars are made for training, but should only be used by experienced handlers and are *only* for use during training, *never* to be left on the dog.

Check the puppy's collar on a daily basis. The collar should be snug but not tight, keeping in mind that puppies grow every hour of the day.

CHOOSE AN APPROPRIATE COLLAR

The **BUCKLE COLLAR** is the standard collar used for everyday purposes. Be sure that you adjust the buckle on growing puppies. Check it every day. It can become too tight overnight! These collars can be made of leather or nylon. Attach your dog's identification tags to this collar.

The **CHOKE COLLAR** is constructed of highly polished steel so that it slides easily through the stainless steel loop. The idea is that the dog controls the pressure around its neck and he will stop pulling if the collar becomes uncomfortable.

The **HALTER** is for a trained dog that has to be restrained to prevent running away, chasing a cat and the like. Considered the most humane of all collars, it is frequently used on smaller dogs for which collars are not comfortable.

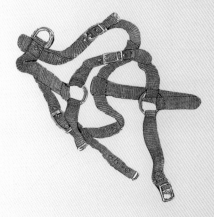

Your local pet shop sells a variety of dishes and bowls for water and food.

Your local pet shop sells a variety of dishes and bowls for water and food.

PHOTO COURTESY OF MIKKI PET PRODUCTS.

FOOD AND WATER BOWLS

Your pup will need two bowls, one for food and one for water. You may want two sets of bowls, one for indoors and one for outdoors, depending on where the dog will be fed and where he will be spending time. Stainless steel or sturdy plastic bowls are popular choices. Plastic bowls are more chewable, but dogs tend not to chew on the steel variety, which can be sterilised. It is important to buy sturdy bowls since anything is in danger of being chewed by puppy teeth and you do not want your dog to be constantly chewing apart his bowl (for his safety and for your purse!).

CLEANING SUPPLIES

Until a pup is house-trained, you will be doing a lot of cleaning. 'Accidents' will occur, which is acceptable in the beginning stages of toilet training because the puppy does not know any better. All you can do is be prepared to clean up any accidents as soon as they happen. Old rags, towels, newspapers and a safe disinfectant are good to have on hand.

BEYOND THE BASICS

The items previously discussed are the bare necessities. You will find out what else you need as you go along—grooming supplies, flea/tick protection, baby gates to partition a room, etc. These things will vary depending on your situation, but it is important that you have everything you need to feed and make your Sealyham comfortable in his first few days at home.

PUPPY-PROOFING YOUR HOME
Aside from making sure that your Sealyham will be comfortable in your home, you also have to make sure that your home is safe for your Sealyham. This means taking precautions that your pup will not get into anything he should not get into and that there is nothing within his reach that may harm him should he sniff it, chew it, inspect it, etc. This probably seems obvious since, while you are primarily concerned with your pup's safety, at the same time you do not want your belongings to be ruined. Breakables should be placed out of reach if your dog is to have full run of the house. If he is to be limited to certain places within the house, keep any potentially dangerous items in the 'off-limits' areas.

An electrical cord can pose a danger should the puppy decide to taste it—and who is going to convince a pup that it would not make a great chew toy? Cords should be fastened tightly against the wall. If your dog is going to spend time in a crate, make sure that there is nothing near his crate that he can reach if he sticks his curious little nose or paws

Be wary of the plants and shrubs that grow around your home, as some of these can be toxic to dogs if eaten accidentally.

through the openings. Just as you would with a child, keep all household cleaners and chemicals where the pup cannot reach them.

It is also important to make sure that the outside of your home is safe. Of course, your puppy should never be unsupervised, but a pup let loose in the garden will want to run and explore, and he should be granted that freedom. Do not let a fence give you a false sense of security; you would be surprised at how crafty (and persistent) a dog can be in working out how to dig under and squeeze his way through small holes, or to jump or climb over a fence. The Sealy, like other terriers, is more likely to dig his way under a fence than to climb or jump over it. The remedy is to make the fence well embedded into the ground and, to be on the safe side, high enough so that it really is impossible for your dog

The wire crate is the most popular style for use in the home. With a cosy wool blanket, your Sealy pup should make himself at home in his crate in no time.

to get over it (about 1.5 metres should suffice). Be sure to repair or secure any gaps in the fence. Check the fence periodically to ensure that it is in good shape and make repairs as needed; a very determined pup may return to the same spot to 'work on it' until he is able to get through.

FIRST TRIP TO THE VET
You have selected your puppy, and your home and family are ready. Now all you have to do is collect your Sealyham from the breeder and the fun begins, right? Well…not so fast. Something else you need to plan is your pup's first trip to the veterinary surgeon. Perhaps the breeder can recommend someone in the area who specialises in terriers, or maybe you know some other Sealyham owners who can suggest a good vet. Either way, you should have an appointment arranged for

Chewing on the lead is great fun for the pup, but must be discouraged immediately.

your pup before you pick him up.

The pup's first visit will consist of an overall examination to make sure that the pup does not have any problems that are not apparent to the eye. The veterinary surgeon will also set up a schedule for the pup's vaccinations; the breeder will inform you of which ones the pup has already received and the vet can continue from there.

INTRODUCTION TO THE FAMILY
Everyone in the house will be excited about the puppy's coming home and will want to pet him and play with him, but it is best to make the introduction low-key so as not to overwhelm the puppy. He is apprehensive already. It is the first time he has been separated from his mother and the breeder, and the ride to your home is likely to be the first time he has been in a car. The last

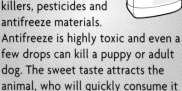

CHEMICAL TOXINS
Scour your garage for potential puppy dangers. Remove weed killers, pesticides and antifreeze materials. Antifreeze is highly toxic and even a few drops can kill a puppy or adult dog. The sweet taste attracts the animal, who will quickly consume it from the floor or kerbside.

thing you want to do is smother him, as this will only frighten him further. This is not to say that human contact is not extremely necessary at this stage, because this is the time when a connection between the pup and his human family is formed. Gentle petting and soothing words should help console him, as well as just putting him down and letting him explore on his own (under your watchful eye, of course).

The pup may approach the family members or may busy himself with exploring for a while. Gradually, each person should spend some time with the pup, one at a time, crouching down to get as close to the pup's level as possible, letting him sniff their hands and petting him gently. He definitely needs human attention and he needs to be touched—this is how to form an immediate bond. Just remember that the pup is experiencing many things for the first time, at the same time. There are new people, new noises, new smells and new things to investigate, so be gentle, be affectionate and be as comforting as you can be.

PUP'S FIRST NIGHT HOME
You have travelled home with your new charge safely in his crate. He's been to the vet for a thorough check-up; he's been weighed, his papers have been examined and perhaps he's even been vaccinated and wormed as well. He's met (and licked!) the whole family, including the excited children and the less-than-happy cat. He's explored his crate, his new bed, the garden and anywhere else he's been permitted. He's eaten his first meal at home and relieved himself in the proper place. He's heard lots of new sounds, smelled new friends and seen more of the outside world than ever before… and that was just the first day! He's worn out and is ready for bed…or so you think!

It's puppy's first night home and you are ready to say 'Good night.' Keep in mind that this is his first night ever to be sleeping alone. His dam and littermates are no longer at paw's length and he's a bit scared, cold and lonely. Be reassuring to your new family member, but this is not the time to spoil him and give in to his inevitable whining.

Puppies whine. They whine to let others know where they are and hopefully to get company out of it. At bedtime, place your pup in his new bed or crate in his designated area and close the door. Mercifully, he may fall asleep without a peep. When the inevitable occurs, however, ignore the whining—he is fine. Be strong and keep his interest in mind. Do not allow yourself to feel guilty and visit the pup. He will fall asleep eventually.

Leaving the breeder's home and his litter-mates, your new puppy may be less outgoing at first than you expect. Given some time, he will warm up to his new environment and socialise with his new family members.

SOCIALISATION PERIOD

The socialisation period for puppies is from age 8 to 16 weeks. This is the time when puppies need to leave their birth family and take up residence with their new owners, where they will meet many new people, other pets, etc. Failure to be adequately socialised can cause the dog to grow up fearing others and being shy and unfriendly due to a lack of self-confidence.

Many breeders recommend placing a piece of bedding from the pup's former home in his new bed so that he recognises and is comforted by the scent of his littermates. Others still advise placing an hot water bottle in the bed for warmth. The latter may be a good idea provided the pup doesn't attempt to suckle—he'll get good and wet, and may not fall asleep so fast.

Puppy's first night can be somewhat stressful for both the pup and his new family. Remember that you are setting the

Sealyham puppies on the move! Like most other dogs, Sealys will follow their noses to the ends of the earth...or the carpet.

tone of night-time at your house. Unless you want to play with your pup every night at 10 p.m., midnight and 2 a.m., don't initiate the habit. Your family will thank you, and so will your pup!

PREVENTING PUPPY PROBLEMS

SOCIALISATION

Now that you have done all of the preparatory work and have helped your pup get accustomed to his new home and family, it is about time for you to have some fun! Socialising your Sealyham pup gives you the opportunity to show off your new friend, and your pup gets to reap the benefits of being an adorable furry creature that people will want to pet and, in general, think is absolutely precious!

Besides getting to know his new family, your puppy should be exposed to other people, animals and situations. This will help him become well adjusted as he grows up and less prone to being timid or fearful of the new things he will encounter. Of course, he must not come into close contact with dogs you don't know well until his course of injections is fully complete.

Your pup's socialisation began with the breeder, but now it is your responsibility to continue it. The socialisation he receives until the age of 12 weeks is the most

critical, as this is the time when he forms his impressions of the outside world. Be especially careful during the eight-to-ten-week-old period, also known as the fear period. The interaction he receives during this time should be gentle and reassuring. Lack of socialisation, and/or negative experiences during the socialisation period, can manifest itself in fear and aggression as the dog grows up. Your puppy needs lots of positive interaction, which of course includes human contact, affection, handling and exposure to other animals. Since Sealys can be slightly aggressive towards other dogs, socialisation is critical at all stages.

Once your pup has received his necessary vaccinations, feel free to take him out and about (on his lead, of course). Walk him around the neighbourhood, take him on your daily errands, let people pet him, let him meet other dogs and pets, etc. Puppies do not have to try to make friends; there will be no shortage of people who will want to introduce themselves. Just make sure that you carefully supervise each meeting. If the neighbourhood children want to say hello, for example, that is great—children and pups most often make great companions. However, sometimes an excited child can unintentionally handle a pup too roughly, or an overzealous pup

MANNERS MATTER
During the socialisation process, a puppy should meet people, experience different environments and definitely be exposed to other canines. Through playing and interacting with other dogs, your puppy will learn lessons, ranging from controlling the pressure of his jaws by biting his littermates to the inner-workings of the canine pack, which he will apply to his human relationships for the rest of his life. That is why removing a puppy from his litter too early (before eight weeks) can be detrimental to the pup's development.

can playfully nip a little too hard. You want to make socialisation experiences positive ones. What a pup learns during this very formative stage will affect his attitude toward future encounters. You want your dog to be comfortable around everyone. A pup that has a bad experience with a child may grow up to be a dog that is shy around or aggressive toward children.

SOCIALISATION TIP

Thorough socialisation includes not only meeting new people but also being introduced to new experiences such as riding in the car, having his coat brushed, hearing the television, walking in a crowd—the list is endless. The more your pup experiences, and the more positive the experiences are, the less of a shock and the less frightening it will be for your pup to encounter new things.

CONSISTENCY IN TRAINING

Dogs, being pack animals, naturally need a leader, or else they try to establish dominance in their packs. When you welcome a dog into your family, the choice of who becomes the leader and who becomes the 'pack' is entirely up to you! Your pup's intuitive quest for dominance, coupled with the fact that it is nearly impossible to look at an adorable Sealyham pup with his 'puppy-dog' eyes and not cave in, give the pup almost an unfair advantage in getting the upper hand! A pup will definitely test the waters to see what he can and cannot do. Do not give in to those pleading eyes—stand your ground when it comes to disciplining the pup and make sure that all family members do the same. It will only confuse the pup if Mother tells him to get off the sofa when he is used to sitting up there with Father to watch the nightly news. Avoid discrepancies by having all members of the household decide on the rules before the pup even comes home... and be consistent in enforcing them! Early training shapes the dog's personality, so you cannot be unclear in what you expect.

COMMON PUPPY PROBLEMS

The best way to prevent puppy problems is to be proactive in stopping an undesirable behaviour as soon as it starts. The old saying 'You can't teach an old dog new tricks' does not necessarily hold true, but it is true that it is much easier to discourage bad behaviour in a young developing pup than to wait until the pup's bad behaviour becomes the adult dog's bad habit. There are some problems that are especially prevalent in puppies as they develop.

NIPPING

As puppies start to teethe, they feel the need to sink their teeth into anything available...unfortunately, that usually includes your fingers, arms, hair and toes. You may find this behaviour cute for the first five seconds...until you feel just how sharp those puppy teeth are. Nipping is something you want to discourage immediately and consistently with a firm 'No!' (or whatever number of firm 'Nos' it takes for him to understand that you mean business). Then, replace your finger with an appropriate chew toy. While this behaviour is merely annoying when the dog is young, it can become dangerous as your Sealyham's adult teeth grow in and his jaws develop, and he continues to think it is okay to gnaw on human appendages. Your Sealyham does not mean any harm with a friendly nip, but he also does not know his own strength.

CHEWING TIPS

Chewing goes hand in hand with nipping in the sense that a teething puppy is always looking for a way to soothe his aching gums. In this case, instead of chewing on you, he may have taken a liking to your favourite shoe or something else which he should not be chewing. Again, realise that this is a normal canine behaviour that does not need to be discouraged, only redirected. Your pup just needs to be taught what is acceptable to chew on and what is off limits. Consistently tell him NO when you catch him chewing on something forbidden and give him a chew toy.

CRYING/WHINING

Your pup will often cry, whine, whimper, howl or make some other type of commotion when he is left alone. This is basically his way of calling out for attention to make sure that you know he is there and that you have not forgotten about him. Your puppy feels insecure when he is left alone, when you are out of the house and he is in his crate or when you are in another part of the house and he cannot see you. The noise he is making is an expression of the anxiety he feels at being alone, so he needs to be taught that being alone is okay. You are not actually training the dog to stop making noise; rather, you are training him to feel comfortable when he is alone and thus removing the need for him to make the noise.

This is where the crate with cosy bedding and a toy comes in handy. You want to know that your pup is safe when you are not there to supervise, and you know that he will be safe in his crate rather than roaming freely about the house. In order for the pup to stay in his crate without making a fuss, he first needs to be comfortable in his crate. On that note, it is extremely important that the crate is never used as a form of punishment; this will cause the pup to view the crate as a negative place, rather than as a place of his own

STRESS-FREE
Some experts in canine health advise that stress during a dog's early years of development can compromise and weaken his immune system, and may trigger the potential for a shortened life expectancy. They emphasise the need for happy and stress-free growing-up years.

for safety and retreat.

Accustom the pup to the crate in short, gradually increasing time intervals in which you put him in the crate, maybe with a treat, and stay in the room with him. If he cries or makes a fuss, do not go to him, but stay in his sight. Gradually he will realise that staying in his crate is all right without your help, and it will not be so traumatic for him when you are not around. You may want to leave the radio on softly when you leave the house; the sound of human voices may be comforting to him.

TEETHING TIP
Puppies like soft toys for chewing. Because they are teething, soft items like stuffed toys soothe their aching gums, but be sure to monitor your pup when he's playing with a potentially destructible (and thus potentially dangerous) toy.

Once your pup accepts the crate as his own safe place, it will become an invaluable tool in warding off separation anxiety. Give him a safe toy and a tasty treat and he will happily settle into his crate until you return.

DIETARY AND FEEDING CONSIDERATIONS

Today the choices of food for your Sealyham Terrier are many and varied. There are simply dozens of brands of food in all sorts of flavours and textures, ranging from puppy diets to those for veterans. There are even hypoallergenic and low-calorie diets available. Because your Sealy's food has a bearing on coat, health and temperament, it is essential that the most suitable diet is selected for a Sealyham of his age. It is fair to say, however, that even experienced owners can be perplexed by the enormous range of foods available. Only understanding what is best for your dog will help you reach an informed decision.

Dog foods are produced in three basic types: dried, semi-moist and tinned. Dried foods are useful for the cost-conscious, for overall they tend to be less expensive than semi-moist or tinned foods. Dried foods also contain the least fat and the most preservatives. In general, tinned foods are made up of 60–70 percent water, while semi-moist ones often contain so much sugar that they are perhaps the least

FOOD STORAGE
You must store your dried dog food carefully. Open packages of dog food quickly lose their vitamin value, usually within 90 days of being opened. Mould spores and vermin also could contaminate the food.

preferred by owners, even though their dogs seem to like them.

When selecting your dog's diet, three stages of development must be considered: the puppy stage, the adult stage and the veteran or senior stage.

PUPPY STAGE

Puppies instinctively want to suck milk from their mother's teats; a normal puppy will exhibit this behaviour just a few moments following birth. If puppies do not attempt to suckle within the first half-hour or so, they should be encouraged to do so by placing them on the nipples, having selected ones with plenty of milk. This early milk supply is important in providing the essential colostrum, which protects the puppies during the first eight to ten weeks of their lives. Although a mother's milk is much better than any milk formula,

TEST FOR PROPER DIET

A good test for proper diet is the colour, odour and firmness of your dog's stool. An healthy dog usually produces three semi-hard stools per day. The stools should have no unpleasant odour. They should be the same colour from excretion to excretion.

FOOD PREFERENCE

Selecting the best dried dog food is difficult. There is no majority consensus among veterinary scientists as to the value of nutrient analyses (protein, fat, fibre, moisture, ash, cholesterol, minerals, etc.). All agree that feeding trials are what matter, but you also have to consider the individual dog. The dog's weight, age and activity level, and what pleases his taste, all must be considered. It is probably best to take the advice of your veterinary surgeon. Every dog's dietary requirements vary, even during the lifetime of a particular dog.

If your dog is fed a good dried food, it does not require supplements of meat or vegetables. Dogs do appreciate a little variety in their diets, so you may choose to stay with the same brand but vary the flavour. Alternatively, you may wish to add a little flavoured stock to give a difference to the taste.

despite there being some excellent ones available, if the puppies do not feed, the breeder will have to feed them by hand. For those with less experience, advice from a veterinary surgeon is important so that not only the right quantity of milk is fed but also that of correct quality, fed at suitably frequent intervals, usually every two hours during the first few days of life.

Puppies should be allowed to nurse from their mothers for about the first six weeks, although, starting around the third or fourth week, the breeder will begin to introduce small portions of suitable solid food. Most breeders like to introduce alternate milk and meat meals initially, building up to weaning time.

By the time the puppies are seven or a maximum of eight weeks old, they should be fully weaned and fed solely on a proprietary puppy food. Selection of the most suitable, good-quality diet at this time is essential, for a puppy's fastest growth rate is during the first year of life. Veterinary surgeons are usually able to offer advice in this regard. The frequency of meals will be reduced over time, and when a young dog has reached the age of about 12 months, he can be switched to an adult diet. Puppy and junior diets should be well balanced for the needs of your dog so that, except in certain circumstances, additional vitamins,

minerals and proteins will not be required.

ADULT DIETS

A dog is considered an adult when it has stopped growing, so in general the diet of a Sealyham can be changed to an adult one at about 12 months of age. Again you should rely upon your veterinary surgeon or dietary specialist to recommend an acceptable maintenance diet. Major dog food manufacturers specialise in this type of food, and it is merely necessary for you to select the one best suited to your dog's needs. Active dogs may have different requirements from sedate dogs.

VETERAN DIETS

As dogs get older, their metabolism changes. The older dog usually exercises less, moves more slowly and sleeps more. This change in lifestyle and physiological performance requires a change in diet. Since these changes take place slowly, they might not be recognisable. What is easily recognisable is weight gain. By continuing to feed your dog an adult-maintenance diet when it is slowing down metabolically, your dog will gain weight. Obesity in an older dog compounds the health problems that already accompany old age.

As your dog gets older, few of his organs function up to par. The kidneys slow down and the intestines become less efficient. These age-related factors are best handled with a change in diet and a change in feeding schedule to give smaller portions that are more easily digested. There is no single best diet for every older dog. While many dogs do well on light or senior diets, other dogs do better on puppy diets or other special premium diets such as lamb and rice. Be sensitive to your senior Sealyham's diet, as this will help control other problems that may arise with your old friend.

GRAIN-BASED DIETS

Some less expensive dog foods are based on grains and other plant proteins. While these products may appear to be attractively priced, breeders prefer a diet based on animal proteins and believe that they are more conducive to your dog's health. Many grain-based diets rely on soy protein, which may cause flatulence (passing gas).

There are many cases, however, when your dog might require a special diet. These special require-ments should only be recommended by your veterinary surgeon.

WATER

Just as your dog needs proper nutrition from his food, water is an essential 'nutrient' as well. Water keeps the dog's body properly hydrated and promotes normal function of the body's systems. During house-training, it is necessary to keep an eye on how much water your Sealyham is drinking, but once he is reliably trained he should have access to clean fresh water at all times, especially if you feed dried food. Make certain that the dog's water bowl is clean, and change the water often.

EXERCISE

Terriers are among the most active of companion dogs, given their seemingly boundless energy and natural vigour. To keep your Sealy in proper condition, daily exercise is a basic requirement for this breed. Regular walks, games and the like will keep your Sealy's legs and mind busy. Never let your Sealy get bored, or he will find undesirable ways of biding his time.

While the Sealyham Terrier is an active breed that enjoys exercise, you don't have to be an

Fresh, clean water is essential to every dog, though you must monitor the amount of water your puppy is drinking during house-training so that you'll know when he needs to 'go.'

Olympic athlete to provide it with a sufficient amount of activity! Exercising your Sealyham can be enjoyable and healthy for both of you. Brisk walks, once the puppy reaches three or four months of age, will stimulate heart rates and build muscle for both dog and owner. As the dog reaches adulthood, the speed and distance of the walks can be increased as long as they are both kept reasonable and comfortable for you and the dog.

Play sessions in the garden and letting the dog run free in the garden under your supervision also are sufficient forms of exercise for the Sealyham. Fetching games can be played indoors or out; these are excellent for giving your dog active play that he will enjoy. Chasing things that move comes naturally to dogs of all breeds. When your Sealyham runs after the ball or object, praise him for picking it up and encourage him to bring it back to you for another throw. Never go to the object and pick it up yourself, or you'll soon find that you are the one retrieving the objects rather than the dog! If you choose to play games outdoors, you must have a securely fenced-in garden and/or have the dog attached to at least an 8-metre (26-foot) light line for security. You want your Sealyham to run, but not run away!

Bear in mind that an overweight dog should never be suddenly over-exercised; instead he should be encouraged to

A Worthy Investment

Veterinary studies have proven
that a balanced high-quality
diet pays off in your dog's coat
quality, behaviour and activity
level. Invest in premium
brands for the maximum
benefit for your dog.

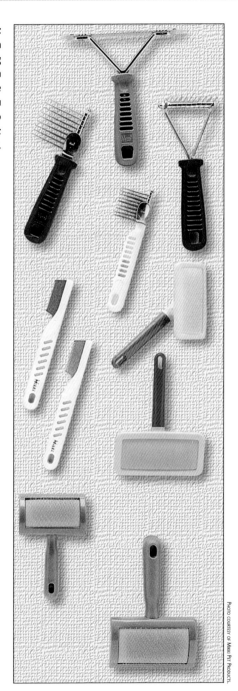

PHOTO COURTESY OF MIKKI PET PRODUCTS.

increase exercise slowly. Not only is exercise essential to keep the dog's body fit, it is essential to his mental well-being. A bored dog will find something to do, which often manifests itself in some type of destructive behaviour. In this sense, exercise is essential for the owner's mental well-being as well!

GROOMING THE SEALY

As desirable as the Sealyham sounds, do be aware when purchasing this breed that there are some grooming issues that you would not have in other breeds. First, there is the problem of a white dog. White dogs will show the wear and tear of their busy lives. Other terriers like Scotties, with their dark coats, and Cairns, with their multicoloured coats, can run up and down the garden and you may not be aware of just how much dirt may be in their coats when you bring them indoors. The Sealyham, on the other hand, particularly if he has been digging, which terriers are prone to do when bored, will truly look a sight as he runs through the door on your clean kitchen floor. If it is a wet and muddy day, he will look even more frightful.

Grooming, a requirement in all breeds, is essential in the Sealyham if you want a dog that you can live with. The Sealy is a double-coated dog. His coat consists of a dense, thick undercoat that protects the dog in all kinds of weather and an harsh outer coat.

Coat care for the pet Sealy can be much different and easier than the coat care for a show dog. The vast majority of Sealy fanciers have their dogs as pets and they should not expect to maintain a show coat. If you are planning to show your Sealyham Terrier, you will be ahead of the game if you purchase your puppy from a reputable breeder who grooms and shows his own dogs. If so, this is the individual to see for grooming lessons to learn how to get your dog ready for the show ring. Grooming for the show ring is an art, and an art that cannot be learned in a few months. Furthermore, it is very difficult—but not impossible—to learn it from a book.

The primary difference between the pet and show coat is that the show Sealy will have a dense undercoat and on top of it he will have a shiny, harsh coat that will fit him like a jacket. With the proper coat, the dog presents a smartness in the ring that is indeed hard to beat. This coat can only be acquired by stripping the body coat with a stripping knife or stripping by hand. Within 10 to 12 weeks, and with the proper upkeep, he will have grown from his 'knickers' stage into a smart new outfit, ready for the ring. This

Use a standard grooming table with a rubber non-slip mat to introduce your pup to the grooming process. Make him feel safe and unthreatened during grooming.

The slicker brush can be used carefully to groom the adult's facial furnishings.

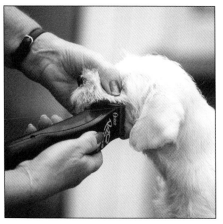

Your breeder can demonstrate for you how to clip the puppy coat. It's best to undertake grooming the Sealyham with the instruction of your breeder or a groomer.

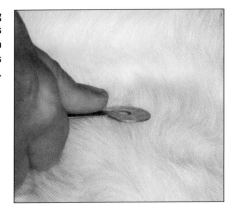

The stripping knife removes dead hair from the Sealyham's coat.

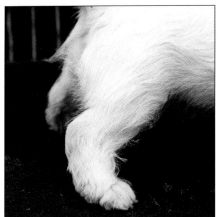

Tidy up the hair around the tail and on the legs with scissors.

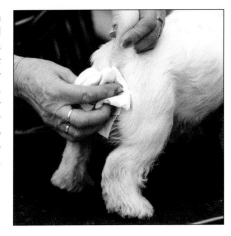

The anal region can be cleaned and the glands checked as a part of your regular grooming process. Ask your vet or breeder to show you how to express the glands.

all takes skill, time and interest in order to do it well.

Pet grooming is different from grooming for the show ring, as you use a clipper on the body and scissors for trimming the furnishings. You will not have the harsh, tight-fitting jacket of the show Sealy, but you will have a neat, clean and trimmed dog that will still look like a Sealyham Terrier. Even those breeders with kennels who are active in the show ring will clip their veteran dogs or those retired from the show ring.

Here are the tools that you will need if you are going to do your own grooming with your pet Sealyham:

1. Grooming table, something sturdy with a rubber mat covering the top. You will need a grooming arm or an hanger. (You can use a table with an eye hook in the ceiling for holding the lead.) Your dog will now be comfortable even if confined and you will be able to work on the dog. Grooming is a very difficult and frustrating job if you try to groom without a table and a grooming arm.
2. Metal comb.
3. Slicker brush.
4. Good, sharp pair of scissors.
5. Toenail trimmer.
6. Electric clippers with a #10 blade.

Let's begin: Set your dog on the table and put the lead around his neck. Hold the lead up behind the dog's ears and keep it taut when you fasten it to the eye hook. Do not walk away and leave your dog unattended, as he can jump from the table and be left dangling from the lead with his feet scrambling around in the air.

Begin with the slicker brush, brushing out the entire coat. Brush the whiskers toward the nose, the body hair toward the tail, the tail up toward the tip of the tail, the leg furnishings up toward the body and the chest hair down toward the table. Hold the dog up by the front legs and gently brush the stomach hair, first toward the head and then back toward the rear. For cleanliness, you may want to take your scissors and trim the area around the penis. With the girls, trim some of the hair around the vulva.

Now that your dog is brushed out, comb through the coat with your metal comb. By now, you have removed a fair amount of dead hair and your dog will already be looking better. You may find some small mats that can be worked out with your fingers or your metal comb. If you brush your dog out every week or so, you will not have much of a problem with mats.

We are now at the stage where you will take your clippers in hand. Your dog will only need to be clipped every three months or

so, but you may want to touch up the head more often. Start with the head and follow this pattern: Take the clippers and clip the neck, shoulders and body, following a pattern from the neck toward the rear and downward to the feet. Be sure to trim in the direction in which the hair lays. Do not undertake this without having a breeder or groomer show you the proper path to clip, or you may transform your Sealy into a Westie, a Scottie or something else altogether!

Next, take your comb and comb the leg hair down toward the table. Take your scissors and trim the legs neatly. With the scissors, trim off anything that sticks out. Speaking of which, be very careful when trimming around the male's penis (and the female's vulva).

If this is your first experience, you may be a bit clumsy, but the hair will grow back in a short time. The finished product may not be quite what you had expected, but expertise will come with experience and you will soon be very proud of your efforts. Your dog should now look like a Sealyham Terrier.

If you have grooming problems, you can take your dog to the professional groomer for his grooming for the first couple of times. A groomer who is familiar with grooming Scottish Terriers will do a very adequate job of

Examine your puppy's mouth regularly and initiate an home dental-care routine to keep your Sealy's teeth and gums clean and healthy.

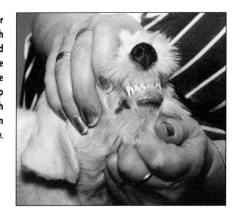

Wipe around the puppy's eyes with a tear-stain remover, available from your pet shop.

Introduce the puppy to having his nails clipped at a young age. Be careful not to cut the 'quick.'

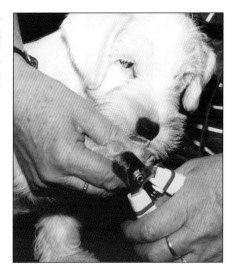

grooming Sealys. The groomer will 'set' the pattern in your dog's coat and then it will be easier for you to get the Sealy look by following the pattern that is already set in the coat. (Of course, you can eliminate all of the grooming for yourself, except for the weekly brushing, if you take your dog to the professional groomer every three months!) If the coat totally grows out before you start to groom, the pattern will be lost and then you will have to start over again.

BATHING

Dogs do not need to be bathed as often as humans, but regular bathing is essential for healthy skin and an healthy, shiny coat. Again, like most anything, if you accustom your pup to being bathed as a puppy, it will be second nature by the time he grows up. You want your dog to be at ease in the bath or else it could end up a wet, soapy, messy ordeal for both of you!

Brush your Sealyham thoroughly before wetting his coat. This will get rid of most mats and tangles, which are harder to remove when the coat is wet. Make certain that your dog has a good non-slip surface on which to stand. Begin by wetting the dog's coat, checking the water temperature to make sure that it is neither too hot nor too cold. A shower or hose attachment is necessary for thoroughly wetting and rinsing the coat.

Next, apply shampoo to the dog's coat and work it into a good lather. Wash the head last, as you do not want shampoo to drip into the dog's eyes while you are washing the rest of his body. You should use only a shampoo that is made for dogs. Do not use a product made for human hair. Work the shampoo all the way down to the skin. You can use this opportunity to check the skin for any bumps, bites or other abnormalities. Do not neglect any area of the body—get all of the hard-to-reach places.

Once the dog has been thoroughly shampooed, he requires an equally thorough rinsing. Shampoo left in the coat can be irritating to the dog's skin. Protect his eyes from the shampoo by shielding them with your hand and directing the flow of water in the opposite direction. You should also avoid getting water in the ear canal. Be prepared for your dog to shake out his coat—you might want to stand back, but make sure you have an hold on the dog to keep him from running through the house. After towelling him down, return him to the grooming table and trim the toenails on all four legs. At this point, you can dry your dog with a blaster and brush him out again, or you can let him dry naturally and then brush him out.

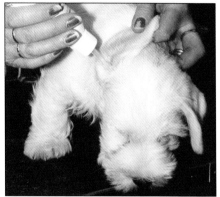

Make ear cleaning part of grooming. If you detect any signs of debris or mites in your pup's ears, alert the vet.

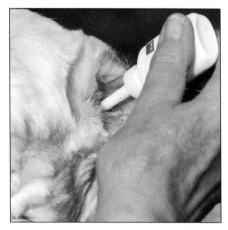

Ear problems in the Sealyham can be a nuisance, though they are manageable with prescribed medication from your vet.

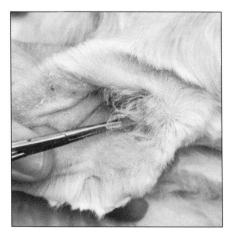

Excess hairs growing inside the ear can be plucked. If done gently, the procedure will be painless for the dog.

Nail Maintenance

Nail Casing

Quick

Cut Line

Dark-Coloured Nails

With black or dark nails, it's best to clip only the tip of the nail or to use a file.

Light-Coloured Nails

In light-coloured nails, clipping is much simpler because you can see the vein (or quick) that grows inside the casing.

EAR CLEANING

The ears should be kept clean with a cotton wipe and ear powder made especially for dogs. Do not probe into the ear canal with a cotton bud, as this can cause injury. Be on the lookout for any signs of infection or ear-mite infestation. If your Sealyham has been shaking his head or scratching at his ears frequently, this usually indicates a problem. If the dog's ears have an unusual odour, this is a sure sign of mite infestation or infection, and a signal to have his ears checked by the veterinary surgeon.

NAIL CLIPPING

Your Sealyham should be accustomed to having his nails trimmed at an early age since nail clipping will be part of your maintenance routine throughout his life. Clip your Sealy's nails at least once per month. A dog's long nails can scratch someone unintentionally and also have a better chance of ripping and bleeding, or causing the feet to spread. A good rule of thumb is that if you can hear your dog's nails' clicking on the floor when he walks, his nails are too long.

Before you start cutting, make sure you can identify the 'quick' in each nail. The quick is a blood vessel that runs through the centre of each nail and grows rather close to the end. The quick will bleed if accidentally cut, which will be quite painful for the dog as it contains nerve endings. Keep some type of clotting agent on hand, such as a styptic pencil or styptic powder (the type used for shaving). This will stop the bleeding quickly when applied to the end of the cut nail. Do not panic if you cut the quick, just stop the bleeding and talk soothingly to your dog. Once he has calmed down, move on to the next nail. It is better to clip a little at a time, particularly with black-nailed dogs.

Hold your pup steady as you begin trimming his nails; you do not want him to make any sudden movements or run away. Talk to him soothingly and stroke him as you clip. Holding his foot in your hand, simply take off the end of each nail with one swift clip. You should purchase nail clippers that are made for use on dogs; you can probably find them wherever you buy pet or grooming supplies.

TRAVELLING WITH YOUR DOG

CAR TRAVEL

You should accustom your Sealyham to riding in a car at an early age. You may or may not take him in the car often, but at the very least he will need to go to

The hair growing on the bottom of your Sealy's foot, around and between the pads, can be tidied up with scissors.

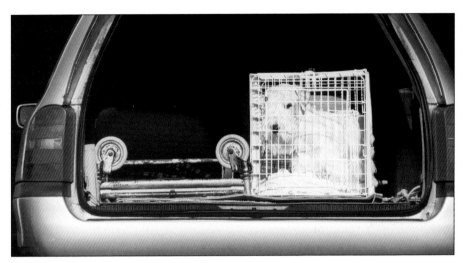

the vet and you do not want these trips to be traumatic for the dog or troublesome for you. The safest way for a dog to ride in the car is in his crate. If he uses a crate in the house, you can use the same crate for travel.

Put the pup in the crate and see how he reacts. If he seems uneasy, you can have a passenger hold him on his lap while you drive. Another option for car travel is a specially made safety harness for dogs, which straps the dog in much like a seat belt. Do not let the dog roam loose in the vehicle—this is very dangerous! If you should stop short, your dog can be thrown and injured. If the dog starts climbing on you and pestering you while you are driving, you will not be able to concentrate on the road. It is an unsafe situation for everyone—human and canine.

For long trips, be prepared to stop to let the dog relieve himself. Take with you whatever you need to clean up after him, including some paper kitchen towels and perhaps some old towelling for use should he have a toileting accident in the car or suffer from travel sickness.

AIR TRAVEL

While it is possible to take a dog on a flight within Britain, this is fairly unusual and advance permission is always required. The dog will be required to travel in a fibreglass crate and you should always check in advance with the airline regarding specific requirements. To help put the dog at ease, give him one of his favourite toys in the crate. Do not feed the dog for several hours before checking in, in order to minimise his need to relieve himself. However, certain regulations specify that water must always be made available to the dog in the crate.

Make sure that your dog is properly identified and that your contact information appears on his ID tags and on his crate. Except for very small pets, animals travel in a different area of the aeroplane from human passengers, so every rule must be strictly followed so as to prevent the risk of getting separated from your dog.

HOLIDAYS AND BOARDING

So you want to take a family holiday—and you want to include *all* members of the family. You would probably make arrangements for accommodation ahead of time anyway, but this is especially important when travelling with a dog. You do not want to make an overnight stop at the only place around for miles, only to find out that they do not allow dogs. Also, you do not want to reserve a place for your family without confirming that you are travelling with a dog, because, if it is against their policy, you may end up without a place to stay.

Alternatively, if you are travelling and choose not to bring your Sealyham, you will have to make arrangements for him while you are away. Some options are to take him to a neighbour's house to stay while you are gone, to

have a trusted neighbour pop in often or stay at your house or to take your dog to a reputable boarding kennel. If you choose to board him at a kennel, you should visit in advance to see the facilities provided and where the dogs are kept. Are the dogs' areas spacious and kept clean? Talk to some of the employees and see how they treat the dogs—do they spend time with the dogs, play with them, exercise them, etc.? Also find out the kennel's policy on vaccinations and what they require. This is for all of the dogs' safety, since there is a greater risk of disease's being passed from dog to dog when dogs are kept together.

IDENTIFICATION

Your Sealyham is your valued companion and friend. That is why you always keep a close eye on him and you have made sure that he cannot escape from the garden or wriggle out of his collar and run away from you. However, accidents can happen and there may come a time when your dog unexpectedly becomes separated from you. If this unfortunate event should occur, the first thing on your mind will be finding him. Proper identification, including an ID tag, a tattoo and possibly a microchip, will increase the chances of his being returned to you safely and quickly.

REAP THE REWARDS

If you start with a normal, healthy dog and give him time, patience and some carefully executed lessons, you will reap the rewards of that training for the life of the dog. And what a life it will be! The two of you will find immeasurable pleasure in the companionship you have built together with love, respect and understanding.

Living with an untrained dog is a lot like owning a piano that you do not know how to play—it is a nice object to look at, but it does not do much more than that to bring you pleasure. Now try taking piano lessons, and suddenly the piano comes alive and brings forth magical sounds and rhythms that set your heart singing and your body swaying.

The same is true with your Sealyham Terrier. Any dog is a big responsibility and, if not trained sensibly, may develop unacceptable behaviour that annoys you or even could cause family friction.

To train your Sealy, you may like to enrol in an obedience class. Teach your dog good manners as you learn how and why he behaves the way he does. Find out how to communicate with your dog and how to recognise and understand his communications with you. Suddenly the dog takes on a new role in your life—he is clever, interesting, well behaved and fun to be with. He demonstrates his bond of devotion to you daily. In other words, your Sealy does wonders for your ego because he constantly reminds you that you are not only his leader, you are his hero!

Those involved with teaching dog obedience and counselling owners about their dogs' behaviour have discovered some interesting facts about dog ownership. For example, training dogs when they are puppies results in the highest rate of success in developing well-mannered and well-adjusted adult dogs. Training an older dog, from six months to six years of age, can produce almost equal results, providing that the owner accepts the dog's slower rate of learning capability and is willing to work patiently to help the dog succeed at developing to his fullest potential. Unfortunately, many owners of untrained adult dogs lack the patience factor, so they do not persist until their dogs are successful at learning particular behaviours.

THE HAND THAT FEEDS

To a dog's way of thinking, your hands are like his mouth in terms of a defence mechanism. If you squeeze him too tightly, he might just bite you because that would be his normal response. This is not aggressive biting and, although all biting should be discouraged, you need the discipline in learning how to handle your dog.

Training a puppy aged 10 to 16 weeks (20 weeks at the most) is like working with a dry sponge in a pool of water. The pup soaks up whatever you show him and constantly looks for more things to do and learn. At this early age, his body is not yet producing hormones, and therein lies the reason for such an high rate of success. Without hormones, he is focused on his owners and not particularly interested in investigating other places, dogs, people, etc. You are his leader: his provider of food, water, shelter and security. He latches onto you and wants to stay close. He will usually follow you from room to room, will not let you out of his sight when you are outdoors with him and will respond in like

Puppies will want to explore everything in their surroundings. Keep your shoes and other tasty distractions away from the ever-curious Sealyham student.

TRAINING TIP
Dogs will do anything for your attention. If you reward the dog when he is calm and resting, you will develop a well-mannered dog. If, on the other hand, you greet your dog excitedly and encourage him to wrestle with you, the dog will greet you the same way and you will have an hyperactive dog on your hands.

manner to the people and animals you encounter. If you greet a friend warmly, he will be happy to greet the person as well. If, however, you are hesitant or anxious about the approach of a stranger, he will respond accordingly.

Once the puppy begins to produce hormones, his natural curiosity emerges and he begins to investigate the world around him. It is at this time when you may notice that the untrained dog begins to wander away from you and even ignore your commands to stay close. When this behaviour becomes a problem, you have two choices: get rid of the dog or train him. It is strongly urged that you choose the latter option.

You usually will be able to find obedience classes within a reasonable distance from your home, but you can also do a lot to train your dog yourself. Sometimes there are classes available, but the tuition is too costly. Whatever the circumstances, the solution to training your dog without obedience classes lies within the pages of this book.

This chapter is devoted to helping you train your Sealyham Terrier at home. If the recommended procedures are followed faithfully, you may expect positive results that will prove rewarding both to you and your dog.

Whether your new charge is a puppy or a mature adult, the

methods of teaching and the techniques we use in training basic behaviours are the same. After all, no dog, whether puppy or adult, likes harsh or inhumane methods. All creatures, however, respond favourably to gentle motivational methods and sincere praise and encouragement. Now let us get started.

TOILET TRAINING

You can train a puppy to relieve himself wherever you choose, but this must be somewhere suitable. You should bear in mind from the outset that when your puppy is old enough to go out in public places, any canine deposits must be removed at once. You will always have to carry with you a small plastic bag or 'poop-scoop.'

Outdoor training includes such surfaces as grass, soil and cement. Indoor training usually means training your dog to newspaper. When deciding on the surface and location that you will want your Sealyham to use, be sure it is going to be permanent. Training your dog to grass and then changing your mind a few months later is extremely difficult for both dog and owner.

Next, choose the command you will use each and every time you want your puppy to void. 'Hurry up' and 'Toilet' are examples of commands commonly used by dog owners. Get in the habit of giving the

MEALTIME
Mealtime should be a peaceful time for your Sealy. Do not put his food and water bowls in an high-traffic area in the house. For example, give him his own little corner of the kitchen where he can eat undisturbed and where he will not be underfoot. Do not allow small children or other family members to disturb the dog when he is eating.

puppy your chosen relief command before you take him out. That way, when he becomes an adult, you will be able to determine if he wants to go out when you ask him. A confirmation will be signs of interest, such as wagging his tail, watching you intently, going to the door, etc.

PUPPY'S NEEDS

Puppy needs to relieve himself after play periods, after each meal, after he has been sleeping and at any time he indicates that he is looking for a place to urinate or defecate. The urinary and intestinal tract muscles of very young puppies are not fully developed. Therefore, like human babies, puppies need to relieve themselves frequently.

Take your puppy out often—every hour for an eight-week-old, for example—and always immediately after sleeping and eating. The older the puppy, the less often he will need to relieve himself. Finally, as a mature healthy adult, he will require only three to five relief trips per day.

HOUSING

Since the types of housing and control you provide for your puppy have a direct relationship on the success of house-training, we consider the various aspects of

Toilet training indoors means accustoming your pup to newspaper. If your home circumstances warrant indoor training, you can teach your pup to use newspaper as his relief area.

THINK BEFORE YOU BARK
Dogs are sensitive to their masters' moods and emotions. Use your voice wisely when communicating with your dog. Never raise your voice at your dog unless you are angry and trying to correct him. 'Barking' at your dog can become as meaningless as 'dogspeak' is to you.

both before we begin training.

Taking a new puppy home and turning him loose in your house can be compared to turning a child loose in a sports arena and telling the child that the place is all his! The sheer enormity of the place would be too much for him to handle. Instead, offer the puppy clearly defined areas where he can play, sleep, eat and live. A room of the house where the family gathers is the most obvious choice. Puppies are social animals and need to feel a part of the pack right from the start. Hearing your voice, watching you while you are doing things and smelling you nearby are all positive reinforcers that he is now a member of your pack. Usually a family room, the kitchen or a nearby adjoining breakfast area is ideal for providing safety and security for both puppy and owner.

Within the designated room, there should be a smaller area that the puppy can call his own. An alcove, a wire or fibreglass dog

CANINE DEVELOPMENT TIMETABLE

It is important to understand how and at what age a puppy develops into adulthood. If you are a puppy owner, consult the following Canine Development Timetable to determine the stage of development your puppy is currently experiencing. This knowledge will help you as you work with the puppy in the weeks and months ahead.

Period	Age	Characteristics
FIRST TO THIRD	BIRTH TO SEVEN WEEKS	Puppy needs food, sleep and warmth, and responds to simple and gentle touching. Needs mother for security and disciplining. Needs littermates for learning and interacting with other dogs. Pup learns to function within a pack and learns pack order of dominance. Begin socialising with adults and children for short periods. Begins to become aware of its environment.
FOURTH	EIGHT TO TWELVE WEEKS	Brain is fully developed. Needs socialising with outside world. Remove from mother and littermates. Needs to change from canine pack to human pack. Human dominance necessary. Fear period occurs between 8 and 12 weeks. Avoid fright and pain.
FIFTH	THIRTEEN TO SIXTEEN WEEKS	Training and formal obedience should begin. Less association with other dogs, more with people, places, situations. Period will pass easily if you remember this is pup's change-to-adolescence time. Be firm and fair. Flight instinct prominent. Permissiveness and over-disciplining can do permanent damage. Praise for good behaviour.
JUVENILE	FOUR TO EIGHT MONTHS	Another fear period about 7 to 8 months of age. It passes quickly, but be cautious of fright and pain. Sexual maturity reached. Dominant traits established. Dog should understand sit, down, come and stay by now.

NOTE: THESE ARE APPROXIMATE TIME FRAMES. ALLOW FOR INDIVIDUAL DIFFERENCES IN PUPPIES.

THE CLEAN LIFE

By providing sleeping and resting quarters that suit the dog, and offering frequent opportunities to relieve himself outside his quarters, the puppy quickly learns that the outdoors (or the newspaper, if you are training him to paper) is the place to go when he needs to urinate or defecate. It also reinforces his innate desire to keep his sleeping quarters clean. This, in turn, helps develop the muscle control that will eventually produce a dog with clean living habits.

small enough so that he cannot relieve himself at one end and sleep at the other without coming into contact with his droppings before he is fully trained to relieve himself outside. Dogs are, by nature, clean animals and will not remain close to their relief areas unless forced to do so. In those cases, they then become dirty dogs and usually remain that way for life.

The dog's designated area should contain clean bedding and a toy. Water must always be available, in a non-spill container, once house-training has been achieved reliably.

CONTROL

By control, we mean helping the puppy to create a lifestyle pattern that will be compatible to that of his human pack (YOU!). Just as we guide little children to learn our way of life, we must show the puppy when it is time to play, eat, sleep, exercise and even entertain himself.

Your puppy should always sleep in his crate. He should also learn that, during times of household confusion and excessive human activity, such as at breakfast when family members are preparing for the day, he can play by himself in relative safety and comfort in his designated area. Each time you leave the puppy alone, he should understand exactly where he is to stay.

crate or a fenced (not boarded!) corner from which he can view the activities of his new family will be fine. The size of the area or crate is the key factor here. The area must be large enough so that the puppy can lie down and stretch out, as well as stand up, without rubbing his head on the top. At the same time, it must be

Puppies are chewers. They cannot tell the difference between lamp and television leads, shoes, table legs, etc. Chewing into a television lead, for example, can be fatal to the puppy, while a shorted wire can start a fire in the house. If the puppy chews on the arm of the chair when he is alone, you will probably discipline him angrily when you get home. Thus, he makes the association that your coming home means he is going to be punished. (He will not remember chewing the chair and is incapable of making the association of the discipline with his naughty deed.) Accustoming the pup to his designated area not only keeps him safe but also avoids his engaging in destructive behaviours when you are not around.

Times of excitement, such as special occasions, family parties, etc., can be fun for the puppy, providing that he can view the activities from the security of his designated area. He is not underfoot and he is not being fed all sorts of titbits that will probably cause him stomach distress, yet he still feels a part of the fun.

SCHEDULE

A puppy should be taken to his relief area each time he is released from his designated area, after meals, after a play session and when he first awakens in the morning (at age eight weeks, this can mean 5 a.m.!). The puppy will indicate that he's ready 'to go' by circling or sniffing busily—do not misinterpret these signs. For a puppy less than ten weeks of age, a routine of taking him out every hour is necessary. As the puppy grows, he will be able to wait for longer periods of time.

Keep trips to his relief area short. Stay no more than five or six minutes and then return to the house. If he goes during that time, praise him lavishly and take him

HONOUR AND OBEY

Dogs are the most honourable animals in existence. They consider another species (humans) as their own. They interface with you. You are their leader. Sealys perceive children to be on their level; their actions around small children are different from their behaviour around their adult masters.

indoors immediately. If he does not, but he has an accident when you go back indoors, pick him up immediately, say 'No! No!' and return to his relief area. Wait a few minutes, then return to the house again. Never hit a puppy or rub his face in urine or excrement after he has had an accident!

Once indoors, put the puppy in his crate until you have had time to clean up his accident. Then, release him to the family

THE SUCCESS METHOD
Success that comes by luck is usually short-lived. Success that comes by well-thought-out proven methods is often more easily achieved and permanent. This is the Success Method. It is designed to give you, the puppy owner, a simple yet proven way to help your puppy develop clean living habits and a feeling of security in his new environment.

THE SUCCESS METHOD
6 Steps to Successful Crate Training

1 Tell the puppy 'Crate time!' and place him in the crate with a small treat (a piece of cheese or half of a biscuit). Let him stay in the crate for five minutes while you are in the same room. Then release him and praise lavishly. Never release him when he is fussing. Wait until he is quiet before you let him out.

2 Repeat Step 1 several times a day.

3 The next day, place the puppy in the crate as before. Let him stay there for ten minutes. Do this several times.

4 Continue building time in five-minute increments until the puppy stays in his crate for 30 minutes with you in the room. Always take him to his relief area after prolonged periods in his crate.

5 Now go back to Step 1 and let the puppy stay in his crate for five minutes, this time while you are out of the room.

6 Once again, build crate time in five-minute increments with you out of the room. When the puppy will stay willingly in his crate (he may even fall asleep!) for 30 minutes with you out of the room, he will be ready to stay in it for several hours at a time.

area and watch him more closely than before. Chances are, his accident was a result of your not picking up his signal or waiting too long before offering him the opportunity to relieve himself. Never hold a grudge against the

Always clean up after your dog, whether you're in a public place or your own garden.

HOW MANY TIMES A DAY?

AGE	RELIEF TRIPS
To 14 weeks	10
14–22 weeks	8
22–32 weeks	6
Adulthood	4
(dog stops growing)	

These are estimates, of course, but they are a guide to the MINIMUM opportunities a dog should have each day to relieve itself.

puppy for accidents.

Let the puppy learn that going outdoors means it is time to relieve himself, not to play. Once trained, he will be able to play indoors and out and still differentiate between the times for play versus the times for relief.

Help him develop regular hours for naps, being alone, playing by himself and just resting, all in his crate. Encourage him to entertain himself while you are busy with your activities. Let him learn that having you near is comforting, but it is not your main purpose in life to provide him with your undivided attention.

Each time you put your puppy in his own area, use the same command, whatever suits best. Soon he will run to his crate or special area when he hears you say those words.

Crate training provides safety for you, the puppy and the home. It also provides the puppy with a feeling of security, and that helps him achieve self-confidence

HOUSE-TRAINING TIP

Most of all, be consistent. Always take your dog to the same location, always use the same command and always have the dog on lead when he is in his relief area, unless a fenced-in garden is available.

By following the Success Method, your puppy will be completely house-trained by the time his muscle and brain development reach maturity. Keep in mind that small breeds usually mature faster than large breeds, but all puppies should be trained by six months of age.

and clean habits. Remember that one of the primary ingredients in house-training your puppy is control. Regardless of your lifestyle, there will always be occasions when you will need to have a place where your dog can stay and be happy and safe. Crate training is the answer for now and

in the future.

In conclusion, a few key elements are really all you need for a successful house-training method—consistency, frequency, praise, control and supervision. By following these procedures with a normal, healthy puppy, you and the puppy will soon be past the stage of 'accidents' and ready to move on to a full and rewarding life together.

ROLES OF DISCIPLINE, REWARD AND PUNISHMENT

Discipline, training one to act in accordance with rules, brings order to life. It is as simple as that. Without discipline, particularly in a group society, chaos will reign supreme and the group will eventually perish. Humans and canines are social animals and need some form of discipline in order to function effectively. They must procure food, protect their home base and their young and reproduce to keep their species going. If there were no discipline

KEEP SMILING

Never train your dog, puppy or adult, when you are angry or in a sour mood. Dogs are very sensitive to human feelings, especially anger, and if your dog senses that you are angry or upset, he will connect your anger with his training and learn to resent or fear his training sessions.

in the lives of social animals, they would eventually die from starvation and/or predation by other stronger animals.

In the case of domestic canines, discipline in their lives is needed in order for them to understand how their pack (you and other family members) functions and how they must act in order to survive.

A large humane society in an highly populated area recently surveyed dog owners regarding their satisfaction with their relationships with their dogs. People who had trained their dogs were 75% more satisfied with

SAFETY FIRST

While it may seem that the most important things to your dog are eating, sleeping and chewing the upholstery on your furniture, his first concern is actually safety. The domesticated dogs we keep as companions have the same pack instinct as their ancestors who ran free thousands of years ago. Because of this pack instinct, your dog wants to know that he and his pack are not in danger of being harmed, and that his pack has a strong, capable leader. You must establish yourself as the leader early on in your relationship. That way your dog will trust that you will take care of him and the pack, and he will accept your commands without question.

their pets than those who had never trained their dogs.

Dr Edward Thorndike, a psychologist, established *Thorndike's Theory of Learning*, which states that a behaviour that results in a pleasant event tends to be repeated. A behaviour that results in an unpleasant event tends not to be repeated. It is this theory upon which training methods are based today. For example, if you manipulate a dog to perform a specific behaviour and reward him for doing it, he is likely to do it again because he enjoyed the end result.

Occasionally, punishment, a penalty inflicted for an offence, is necessary. The best type of punishment often comes from an outside source. For example, a

Your puppy must know the house rules before he invents his own brand of mischief in your home. A puppy's curiosity can lead him into dangerous and destructive behaviour.

FEAR AGGRESSION

Pups who are subjected to physical abuse during training commonly end up with behavioural problems as adults. One common result of abuse is fear aggression, in which a dog will lash out, bare his teeth, snarl and finally bite someone by whom he feels threatened. For example, your daughter may be playing with the dog one afternoon. As they play hide-and-seek, she backs the dog into a corner and, as she attempts to tease him playfully, he bites her hand. Examine the cause of this behaviour. Did your daughter ever hit the dog? Did someone who resembles your daughter hit or scream at the dog?

Fortunately, fear aggression is relatively easy to correct. Have your daughter engage in only positive activities with the dog, such as feeding, petting and walking. She should not give any corrections or negative feedback. If the dog still growls or cowers away from her, allow someone else to accompany them. After approximately one week, the dog should feel that he can rely on her for many positive things, and he will also be prevented from reacting fearfully towards anyone who might resemble her.

child is told not to touch the cooker because he may get burned. He disobeys and touches the cooker. In doing so, he receives a burn. From that time on, he respects the heat of the cooker and avoids contact with it. Therefore, a behaviour that results in an unpleasant event tends not to be repeated.

A good example of a dog learning the hard way is the dog who chases the house cat. He is told many times to leave the cat alone, yet he persists in teasing the cat. Then, one day, the dog begins chasing the cat but the cat turns and swipes a claw across the dog's face, leaving the dog with a painful gash on his nose. The final result is that the dog stops chasing the cat. Again, a behaviour that results in

an unpleasant event tends not to be repeated.

TRAINING EQUIPMENT

COLLAR AND LEAD

For a Sealyham, the collar and lead that you use for training must be one with which you are easily able to work, not too heavy for the dog and perfectly safe.

TREATS

Have a bag of treats on hand; something nutritious and easy to swallow works best. Use a soft treat, a chunk of cheese or a piece of cooked chicken rather than a dry biscuit. By the time the dog has finished chewing a dry treat, he will forget why he is being rewarded in the first place!

Using food rewards will not teach a dog to beg at the table—the only way to teach a dog to beg at the table is to give him food from the table. In training, rewarding the dog with a food treat will help him associate praise and the treats with learning new behaviours that obviously please his owner.

TRAINING BEGINS: ASK THE DOG A QUESTION

In order to teach your dog anything, you must first get his attention. After all, he cannot learn anything if he is looking away from you with his mind on something else.

To get your dog's attention, ask him 'School?' and immediately walk over to him and give him a treat as you tell him 'Good dog.' Wait a minute or two and repeat the routine, this time with a treat in your hand as you approach within a foot of the dog. Do not go directly to him, but stop about a foot short of him and hold out the treat as you ask 'School?' He will see you approaching with a treat in your hand and most likely begin walking toward you. As you meet, give him the treat and praise again.

The third time, ask the question, have a treat in your hand and walk only a short distance toward the dog so that he must walk almost all the way to you. As he reaches you, give him the treat and praise again.

By this time, the dog will probably be getting the idea that if he pays attention to you, especially when you ask that

'NO' MEANS 'NO!'

Dogs do not understand our language. They can be trained to react to a certain sound, at a certain volume. If you say 'No, Oliver' in a very soft pleasant voice, it will not have the same meaning as 'No, Oliver!!' when you shout it as loud as you can. You should never use the dog's name during a reprimand, just the command NO!!

Since dogs don't understand words, comics often use dogs trained with opposite meanings. Thus, when the comic commands his dog to sit the dog will stand up, and vice versa.

Using a treat is the easiest way to convince a Sealy puppy to pay attention to the lesson at hand.

question, it will pay off in treats and enjoyable activities for him. In other words, he learns that 'school' means doing great things with you that are fun and that result in positive attention for him.

Remember that the dog does not understand your verbal language; he only recognises sounds. Your question translates to a series of sounds for him, and those sounds become the signal to go to you and pay attention. The dog learns that if he does this, he will get to interact with you plus receive treats and praise.

THE BASIC COMMANDS

TEACHING SIT

Now that you have the dog's attention, attach his lead and hold it in your left hand, and hold a food treat in your right hand.

Place your food hand at the dog's nose and let him lick the treat but not take it from you. Say 'Sit' and slowly raise your food hand from in front of the dog's nose up over his head so that he is looking at the ceiling. As he bends his head upward, he will have to bend his knees to maintain his balance. As he bends his knees, he will assume a sit position. At that point, release the food treat and praise lavishly with comments such as 'Good dog! Good sit!,' etc. Remember to always praise enthusiastically, because dogs relish verbal praise from their owners and feel so proud of themselves whenever they accomplish a behaviour.

You will not use food forever in getting the dog to obey your commands. Food is only used to teach new behaviours and, once the dog knows what you want when you give a specific command, you will wean him off the food treats but still maintain the verbal praise. After all, you will always have your voice with you, and there will be many times when you have no food rewards but expect the dog to obey.

Teaching Down

Teaching the down exercise is easy when you understand how the dog perceives the down position, and it is very difficult when you do not. Dogs perceive the down position as a submissive one; therefore, teaching the down exercise by using a forceful method can sometimes make the dog develop such a fear of the down that he either runs away when you say 'Down' or he attempts to snap at the person who tries to force him down.

Have the dog sit close alongside your left leg, facing in the same direction as you are. Hold the lead in your left hand and a food treat in your right. Now place your left hand lightly on the top of the dog's shoulders where they meet above the spinal cord. Do not push down on the dog's shoulders; simply rest your left hand there so you can guide the dog to lie down close to your left leg rather than to swing away from your side when he drops.

Now place the food hand at the dog's nose, say 'Down' very softly (almost a whisper), and

PARENTAL GUIDANCE
Training a dog is a life experience. Many parents admit that much of what they know about raising children they learned from caring for their dogs. Dogs respond to love, fairness and guidance, just as children do. Become a good dog owner and you may become an even better parent.

slowly lower the food hand to the dog's front feet. When the food hand reaches the floor, begin moving it forward along the floor in front of the dog. Keep talking softly to the dog, saying things like, 'Do you want this treat? You can do this, good dog.' Your reassuring tone of voice will help calm the dog as he tries to follow the food hand in order to get the treat.

The sit exercise is commonly the first obedience lesson that dog owners undertake. With practice, the Sealy can learn this command in a couple of short lessons.

When the dog's elbows touch the floor, release the food and praise softly. Try to get the dog to maintain that down position for several seconds before you let him sit up again. The goal here is to get the dog to settle down and not feel threatened in the down position.

TEACHING STAY

It is easy to teach the dog to stay in either a sit or a down position. Again, we use food and praise during the teaching process as we help the dog to understand exactly what it is that we are expecting him to do.

To teach the sit/stay, start with the dog sitting on your left side as before and hold the lead in your left hand. Have a food treat in your right hand and place your food hand at the dog's nose. Say 'Stay' and step out on your right foot to stand directly in front of the dog, toe to toe, as he licks and nibbles the treat. Be sure to keep

PLAN TO PLAY

In addition to training sessions, your Sealy should also have regular play and exercise sessions when he is with you or a family member. Exercise for a very young puppy can consist of a short walk around the house or garden. Playing can include fetching games with a large ball or a special raggy. Remember to restrict play periods to indoors within his living area (the family room, for example) until he is completely house-trained.

his head facing upward to maintain the sit position. Count to five and then swing around to stand next to the dog again with him on your left. As soon as you get back to the original position, release the food and praise lavishly.

To teach the down/stay, do the down as previously described. As soon as the dog lies down, say 'Stay' and step out on your right foot just as you did in the sit/stay. Count to five and then return to stand beside the dog with him on your left side. Release the treat and praise as always.

Within a week or ten days, you can begin to add a bit of distance between you and your dog when you leave him. When you do, use your left hand open with the palm facing the dog as a stay signal, much the same as the hand signal a constable uses to stop traffic at a cross roads. Hold the food treat in your right hand as before, but this time the food will not be touching the dog's nose. He will watch the food hand and quickly learn that he is going to get that treat as soon as you return to his side.

When you can stand 1 metre away from your dog for 30 seconds, you can then begin building time and distance in both stays. Eventually, the dog can be expected to remain in the stay position for prolonged periods of time until you return to

DOUBLE JEOPARDY
A dog in jeopardy never lies down. He stays alert on his feet because instinct tells him that he may have to run away or fight for his survival. Therefore, if a dog feels threatened or anxious, he will not lie down. Consequently, it is important to have the dog calm and relaxed as he learns the down exercise.

him or call him to you. Always praise lavishly when he stays.

TEACHING COME
If you make teaching 'come' an exciting experience, you should never have a 'student' that does not love the game or that fails to

celebrate the dog's finding him with a treat and lots of happy praise. When a person calls the dog, he is actually inviting the dog to find him and to get a treat as a reward for 'winning.'

A few turns of the 'Where are you?' game and the dog will understand that everyone is playing the game and that each person has a big celebration awaiting the dog's success at locating him or her. Once the dog learns to love the game, simply

Choose a training location that is devoid of distractions, or else you will be competing for your Sealy's attention.

come when called. The secret, it seems, is never to teach the word 'come.'

At times when an owner most wants his dog to come when called, the owner is likely to be upset or anxious and he allows these feelings to come through in the tone of his voice when he calls his dog. Hearing that desperation in his owner's voice, the dog fears the results of going to him and therefore either disobeys outright or runs in the opposite direction. The secret, therefore, is to teach the dog a game and, when you want him to come to you, simply play the game. It is practically a no-fail solution!

To begin, have several members of your family take a few food treats and each go into a different room in the house. Everyone takes turns calling the dog, and each person should

'WHERE ARE YOU?'

When calling the dog, do not say 'Come.' Say things like, 'Rover, where are you? See if you can find me! I have a biscuit for you!' Keep up a constant line of chatter with coaxing sounds and frequent questions such as, 'Where are you?' The dog will learn to follow the sound of your voice to locate you and receive his reward.

'COME' ... BACK

Never call your dog to come to you for a correction or scold him when he reaches you. That is the quickest way to turn a 'Come' command into 'Go away fast!' Dogs think only in the present tense, and your dog will connect the scolding with coming to you, not with the misbehaviour of a few moments earlier.

TEACHING HEEL

Heeling means that the dog walks beside the owner without pulling. It takes time and patience on the owner's part to succeed at teaching the dog that he (the owner) will not proceed unless the dog is walking calmly beside him. Neither pulling out ahead on the lead nor lagging behind is acceptable.

Begin by holding the lead in your left hand as the dog sits beside your left leg. Move the loop end of the lead to your right hand, but keep your left hand short on the lead so that it keeps the dog in close next to you.

Say 'Heel' and step forward on your left foot. Keep the dog close to you and take three steps. Stop and have the dog sit next to you in what we now call the 'heel position.' Praise verbally, but do not touch the dog. Hesitate a moment and begin again with

calling out 'Where are you?' will bring him running from wherever he is when he hears that all-important question.

The come command is recognised as one of the most important things to teach a dog, but there are trainers who work with thousands of dogs and never teach the actual word 'come.' Yet these dogs will race to respond to a person who uses the dog's name followed by 'Where are you?' For example, a woman has a 12-year-old companion dog who went blind, but who never fails to locate her owner when asked, 'Where are you?'

Children, in particular, love to play this game with their dogs. Children can hide in smaller places like a shower or bath, behind a bed or under a table. The dog needs to work a little bit harder to find these hiding places, but, when he does, he loves to celebrate with a treat and a tussle with a favourite youngster.

'Where are you?' exclaimed in an excited voice, punctuated by some hand clapping, will have your Sealy running to find you.

'Heel,' taking three steps and stopping, at which point the dog is told to sit again.

Your goal here is to have the dog walk those three steps without pulling on the lead. Once he will walk calmly beside you for three steps without pulling, increase the number of steps you take to five. When he will walk politely beside you while you take five steps, you can increase the length of your walk to ten steps. Keep increasing the length of your stroll until the dog will walk quietly beside you without pulling as long as you want him to heel. When you stop heeling, indicate to the dog that the exercise is over by verbally praising as you pet him and say 'OK, good dog.' The 'OK' is used as a release word, meaning that the exercise is finished and the dog is free to relax.

If you are dealing with a dog who insists on pulling you around, simply 'put on your brakes' and stand your ground until the dog realises that the two of you are not going anywhere until he is beside you and moving at your pace, not his. It may take some time just standing there to convince the dog that you are the leader and that you will be the one to decide on the direction and speed of your travel.

Each time the dog looks up at you or slows down to give a slack lead between the two of you,

CONSISTENCY PAYS OFF
Dogs need consistency in their feeding times, exercise and toilet breaks and the verbal commands you use. If you use 'Stay' on Monday and 'Stay here, please' on Tuesday, you will confuse your dog. Don't demand perfect behaviour during training classes and then let him have the run of the house the rest of the day. Above all, lavish praise on your pet consistently every time he does something right. The more he feels he is pleasing you, the more willing he will be to learn.

quietly praise him and say, 'Good heel. Good dog.' Eventually, the dog will begin to respond and within a few days he will be walking politely beside you without pulling on the lead. At first, the training sessions should be kept short and very positive; soon the dog will be able to walk nicely with you for increasingly longer distances. Remember also to give the dog free time and the opportunity to run and play when you have finished heel practice.

WEANING OFF FOOD IN TRAINING
Food is used in training new behaviours. Once the dog understands what behaviour goes with a specific command, it is time to start weaning him off the food treats. At first, give a treat

after each exercise. Then, start to give a treat only after every other exercise. Mix up the times when you offer a food reward and the times when you only offer praise so that the dog will never know when he is going to receive both food and praise and when he is going to receive only praise. This is called a variable ratio reward system. It proves successful because there is always the chance that the owner will produce a treat, so the dog never stops trying for that reward. No matter what, *always* give verbal praise.

OBEDIENCE CLASSES

It is a good idea to enrol in an obedience class if one is available in your area. If yours is a show dog, ringcraft classes would be more appropriate. Many areas have dog clubs that offer basic obedience training as well as preparatory classes for obedience competition. There are also local dog trainers who offer similar classes.

At obedience shows, dogs can earn titles at various levels of competition. The beginning levels of obedience competition include basic behaviours such as sit, down, heel, etc. The more advanced levels of competition include jumping, retrieving, scent discrimination and signal work. The advanced levels require a dog and owner to put a lot of time and

TUG OF WALK?
If you begin teaching the heel by taking long walks and letting the dog pull you along, he misinterprets this action as an acceptable form of taking a walk. When you pull back on the lead to counteract his pulling, he reads that tug as a signal to pull even harder!

effort into their training. The titles that can be earned at these levels of competition are very prestigious.

OTHER ACTIVITIES FOR LIFE

Whether a dog is trained in the structured environment of a class

With proper
instruction and
enough patience,
your Sealyham
Terrier will
become a
reliable, obedient
companion. Don't
neglect your
Sealy's education!

COMMAND STANCE
Stand up straight and authoritatively when giving your dog commands. Do not issue commands when lying on the floor or lying on your back on the sofa. If you are on your hands and knees when you give a command, your dog will think you are positioning yourself to play.

or alone with his owner at home, there are many activities that can bring fun and rewards to both owner and dog once they have mastered basic control.

Teaching the dog to help out around the home, in the garden or on the farm provides great satisfaction to both dog and owner. In addition, the dog's help makes life a little easier for his owner and raises his stature as a valued companion to his family. It helps give the dog a purpose by occupying his mind and providing an outlet for his energy.

If you are interested in participating in organised competition with your Sealyham, there are activities other than obedience in which you and your dog can become involved. Of course, all terriers delight in going-to-ground activities, which may be sponsored by the breed club in your area. More common for all breeds, agility is a popular sport in which dogs run through an

obstacle course that includes various jumps, tunnels and other exercises to test the dog's speed and co-ordination. Mini-agility has been devised by The Kennel Club for small breeds. The events are essentially the same, except all obstacles have been reduced in size so that small dogs can participate. The owners run beside their dogs to give commands and to guide them through the course. Although competitive, the focus is on fun—it's fun to do, fun to watch and great exercise.

THE STUDENT'S STRESS TEST
During training sessions you must be able to recognise signs of stress in your dog such as:
- tucking his tail between his legs
- lowering his head
- shivering or trembling
- standing completely still or running away
- panting and/or salivating
- avoiding eye contact
- flattening his ears back
- urinating submissively
- rolling over and lifting a leg
- grinning or baring teeth
- aggression when restrained

If your four-legged student displays these signs, he may just be nervous or intimidated. The training session may have been too lengthy, with not enough praise and affirmation. Stop for the day and try again tomorrow.

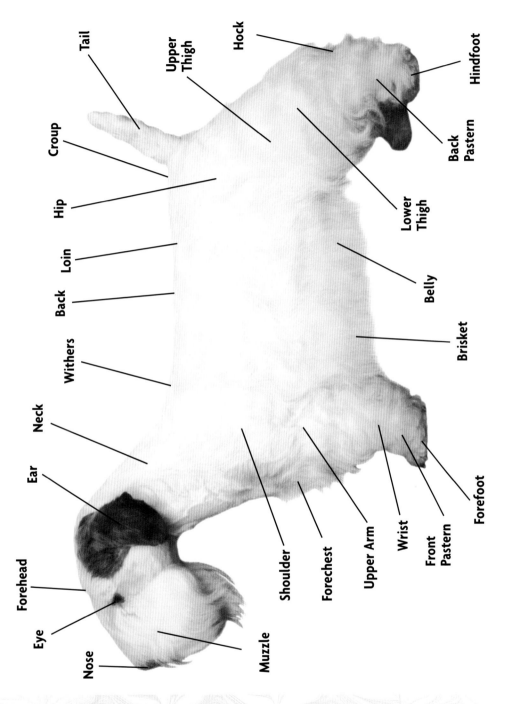

Tail

Upper Thigh

Hock

Croup

Hindfoot

Hip

Back Pastern

Loin

Lower Thigh

Back

Belly

Withers

Brisket

Neck

Ear

Forehead

Forefoot

Eye

Front Pastern

Wrist

Upper Arm

Nose

Forechest

Shoulder

Muzzle

PHYSICAL STRUCTURE OF THE SEALYHAM TERRIER

Dogs suffer from many of the same physical illnesses as people and might even share many of the same psychological problems. Since people usually know more about human diseases than canine maladies, many of the terms used in this chapter will be familiar but not necessarily those used by veterinary surgeons. For example, we will use the familiar term *x-ray* instead of *radiograph*. We will also use the familiar term *symptoms*, even though dogs don't have symptoms, which are verbal descriptions of something the patient feels or observes himself that he regards as abnormal. Dogs have *clinical signs* since they cannot speak, so we have to look for these clinical signs...but we still use the term *symptoms* in the book.

Medicine is a constantly changing art, with some scientific input as well. Things alter as we learn more and more about basic sciences such as genetics and biochemistry, and have use of more sophisticated imaging techniques like Computer Aided Tomography (CAT scans) or Magnetic Resonance Imaging (MRI scans). There is academic dispute about many canine maladies, so different veterinary surgeons treat them in different ways, and some vets place a greater emphasis on surgical techniques than others.

SELECTING A VETERINARY SURGEON
Your selection of a veterinary surgeon should be based on personal recommendation for their skills with small animals, especially dogs, and, if possible, terriers. If the vet is based nearby, it will be helpful because you might have an emergency or need to make multiple visits for treatments.

All veterinary surgeons are licenced, and in Britain are Members of the Royal College of Veterinary Surgeons (MRCVS after their name). The high street veterinary practice deals with routine medical issues such as infections, injuries and the promotion of good health (for example, by vaccination). If the problem affecting your dog is more complex, in Britain your vet will refer your pet to someone with a more detailed knowledge of what is wrong. This usually will be a specialist at the nearest university veterinary school who is a veterinary dermatologist, veterinary ophthalmologist, etc.; whatever is the relevant field.

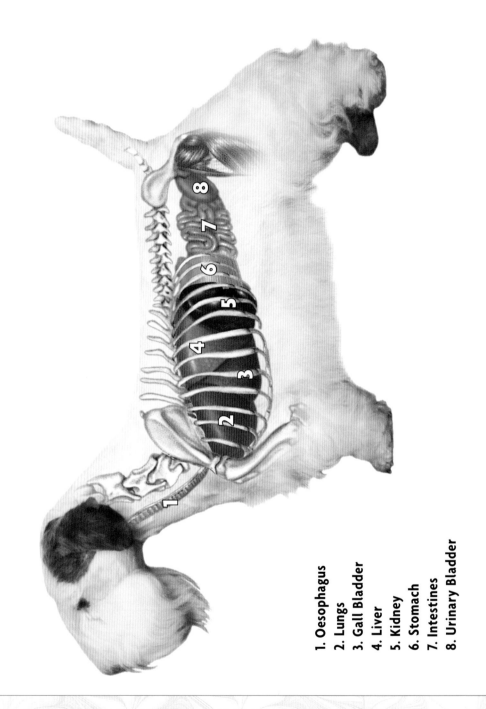

1. Oesophagus
2. Lungs
3. Gall Bladder
4. Liver
5. Kidney
6. Stomach
7. Intestines
8. Urinary Bladder

INTERNAL ORGANS OF THE SEALYHAM TERRIER

Veterinary procedures are very costly and as the treatments available improve, they are going to become more expensive. It is quite acceptable to discuss matters of cost with your vet; if there is more than one treatment option, cost may be a factor in deciding which route to take.

Insurance against veterinary cost is also becoming very popular. This will not pay for routine vaccinations, but will cover the costs for unexpected emergencies such as emergency surgery after a road-traffic accident.

PREVENTATIVE MEDICINE

It is much easier, less costly and more effective to practise preventative medicine than to fight bouts of illness and disease. Properly bred puppies of all breeds come from parents that were selected based upon their genetic disease profile. The puppies' mother should have been vaccinated, free of all internal and external parasites and properly nourished. For these reasons, a visit to the veterinary surgeon who cared for the dam (mother) is recommended if at all possible. The dam passes disease resistance to her puppies, which should last from eight to ten weeks. Unfortunately, she can also pass on parasites and infection. This is why knowledge about her health is useful in learning more about the health of the puppies.

Breakdown of Veterinary Income by Category

2%	Dentistry
4%	Radiology
12%	Surgery
15%	Vaccinations
19%	Laboratory
23%	Examinations
25%	Medicines

A typical American vet's income, categorised according to services performed. This survey dealt with small-animal (pets) practices.

WEANING TO FIVE MONTHS OLD
Puppies should be weaned by the time they are two months old. A puppy that remains for at least eight weeks with its mother and littermates usually adapts better to other dogs and people later in its life.

The new owner should have his puppy examined by a veterinary surgeon immediately, which is a good idea unless the puppy is overtired by a long journey. Vaccination programmes usually begin when the puppy is very young.

The puppy will have its teeth examined and have its skeletal conformation and general health checked prior to certification by the veterinary surgeon. Puppies in certain breeds have problems with their kneecaps, eye cataracts and other eye problems, heart murmurs and undescended

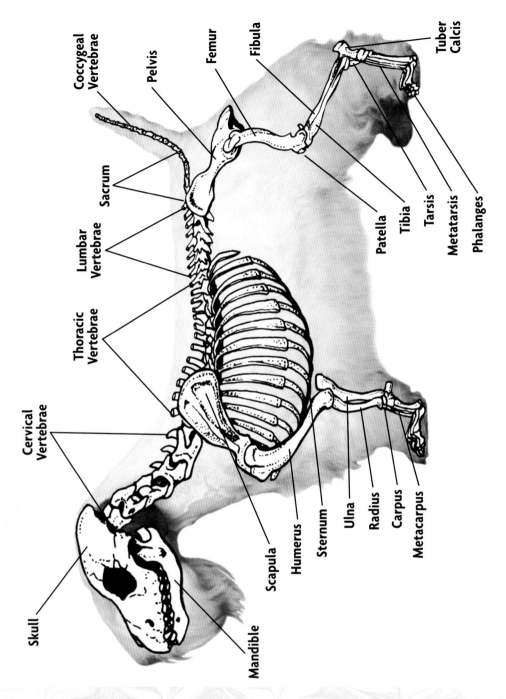

Coccygeal Vertebrae

Pelvis

Femur

Fibula

Tuber Calcis

Sacrum

Patella

Tibia

Tarsis

Metatarsis

Phalanges

Lumbar Vertebrae

Thoracic Vertebrae

Cervical Vertebrae

Skull

Mandible

Scapula

Humerus

Sternum

Ulna

Radius

Carpus

Metacarpus

SKELETAL STRUCTURE OF THE SEALYHAM TERRIER

testicles. They may also have personality problems and your veterinary surgeon might have training in temperament evaluation.

VACCINATIONS

Most vaccinations are given by injection and should only be given by a veterinary surgeon. Both he and you should keep a record of the date of the injection, the identification of the vaccine and the amount given. Some vets give a first vaccination at eight weeks, but most dog breeders prefer the course not to commence until about ten weeks because of interaction with the antibodies produced by the mother. The vaccination programme is usually based on a 15-day cycle. You must take your vet's advice as to when to vaccinate, as this may differ according to the vaccine used.

The usual vaccines contain immunising doses of several different viruses such as distemper, parvovirus, parainfluenza and hepatitis. There are other vaccines available when the puppy is at risk. You should rely upon professional advice. This is especially true for the booster immunisations. Most vaccination programmes require a booster when the puppy is a year

HEALTH AND VACCINATION TIMETABLE

AGE IN WEEKS:	6TH	8TH	10TH	12TH	14TH	16TH	20-24TH	52ND
Worm Control	✔	✔	✔	✔	✔	✔	✔	
Neutering								✔
Heartworm		✔		✔		✔	✔	
Parvovirus	✔		✔		✔		✔	✔
Distemper		✔		✔		✔		✔
Hepatitis		✔		✔		✔		✔
Leptospirosis								✔
Parainfluenza	✔		✔		✔			✔
Dental Examination		✔					✔	✔
Complete Physical		✔					✔	✔
Coronavirus				✔			✔	✔
Kennel Cough	✔							
Hip Dysplasia								✔
Rabies							✔	

Vaccinations are not instantly effective. It takes about two weeks for the dog's immune system to develop antibodies. Most vaccinations require annual booster shots. Your veterinary surgeon should guide you in this regard.

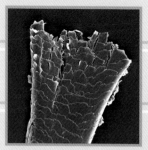

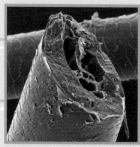

Normal hairs of a dog enlarged 200 times original size. The cuticle (outer covering) is clean and healthy. Unlike human hair that grows from the base, a dog's hair also grows from the end. Damaged hairs and split ends, illustrated above.

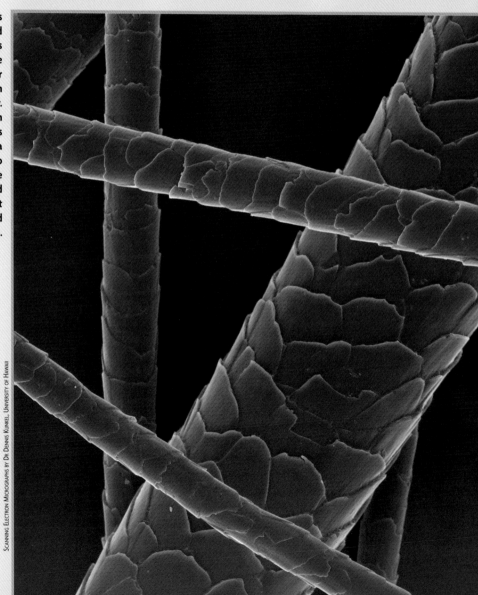

DISEASE REFERENCE CHART

	What is it?	What causes it?	Symptoms
Leptospirosis	Severe disease that affects the internal organs; can be spread to people.	A bacterium, which is often carried by rodents, that enters through mucous membranes and spreads quickly throughout the body.	Range from fever, vomiting and loss of appetite in less severe cases to shock, irreversible kidney damage and possibly death in most severe cases.
Rabies	Potentially deadly virus that infects warm-blooded mammals. Not seen in United Kingdom.	Bite from a carrier of the virus, mainly wild animals.	1st stage: dog exhibits change in behaviour, fear. 2nd stage: dog's behaviour becomes more aggressive. 3rd stage: loss of coordination, trouble with bodily functions.
Parvovirus	Highly contagious virus, potentially deadly.	Ingestion of the virus, which is usually spread through the faeces of infected dogs.	Most common: severe diarrhoea. Also vomiting, fatigue, lack of appetite.
Kennel cough	Contagious respiratory infection.	Combination of types of bacteria and virus. Most common: *Bordetella bronchiseptica* bacteria and parainfluenza virus.	Chronic cough.
Distemper	Disease primarily affecting respiratory and nervous system.	Virus that is related to the human measles virus.	Mild symptoms such as fever, lack of appetite and mucous secretion progress to evidence of brain damage, 'hard pad.'
Hepatitis	Virus primarily affecting the liver.	Canine adenovirus type I (CAV-1). Enters system when dog breathes in particles.	Lesser symptoms include listlessness, diarrhoea, vomiting. More severe symptoms include 'blue-eye' (clumps of virus in eye).
Coronavirus	Virus resulting in digestive problems.	Virus is spread through infected dog's faeces.	Stomach upset evidenced by lack of appetite, vomiting, diarrhoea.

old and once a year thereafter. In some cases, circumstances may require more frequent immunisations.

Kennel cough, more formally known as tracheobronchitis, is immunised against with a vaccine that is sprayed into the dog's nostrils. Kennel cough is usually included in routine vaccination, but it is often not as effective as the vaccines for other major diseases.

FIVE MONTHS TO ONE YEAR OF AGE

Unless you intend to breed or show your dog, neutering the puppy at six months of age is recommended. Discuss this with your veterinary surgeon. Neutering/spaying has proven to be extremely beneficial to male and female puppies, respectively. Besides eliminating the possibility of pregnancy, it inhibits (but does not prevent) breast cancer in bitches and prostate cancer in male dogs. Under no circumstances should a bitch be spayed prior to her first season.

Your veterinary surgeon should provide your puppy with a thorough dental evaluation at six months of age, ascertaining whether all the permanent teeth have erupted properly. An home

dental-care regimen should be initiated at six months, including brushing weekly and providing good dental devices (such as nylon bones). Regular dental care promotes healthy teeth, fresh breath and a longer life.

DOGS OLDER THAN ONE YEAR

Continue to visit the veterinary surgeon at least once a year. There is no such disease as 'old age,' but bodily functions do change with age. Most veterinary surgeons use the seven-year mark to consider a dog a 'senior' or 'veteran.' In an older dog, the eyes and ears are no longer as efficient. Liver, kidney and intestinal functions often decline. Proper dietary changes, recommended by your veterinary surgeon, can make life more pleasant for your ageing Sealyham and you.

SKIN PROBLEMS

Veterinary surgeons are consulted by dog owners for skin problems more than for any other group of diseases or maladies, and the Sealy, unfortunately, frequently suffers from skin allergies and other problems. A dog's skin is as sensitive, if not more so, than human skin, and both suffer almost the same ailments (though the occurrence of acne in dogs is rare!). For this reason, veterinary dermatology has developed into a speciality practised by many veterinary surgeons.

Since many skin problems have visual symptoms that are almost identical, it requires the skill of an experienced veterinary dermatologist to identify and cure many of the more severe skin disorders. Pet shops sell many treatments for skin problems, but most of the treatments are directed at symptoms and not at the underlying problem(s). If your dog is suffering from a skin disorder, you should seek professional assistance as quickly as possible. As with all diseases, the earlier a problem is identified and treated, the better the chance that the cure will be successful.

HEREDITARY SKIN DISORDERS

Veterinary dermatologists are currently researching a number of skin disorders that are believed to have an hereditary basis. These inherited diseases are transmitted

---

Among the hereditary skin disorders, for which the mode of inheritance is known, are acrodermatitis, cutaneous asthenia (Ehlers-Danlos syndrome), sebaceous adenitis, cyclic hematopoiesis, dermatomyositis, IgA deficiency, colour dilution alopaecia and nodular dermatofibrosis. Some of these disorders are limited to one or two breeds, while others affect a large number of breeds. All inherited diseases must be diagnosed and treated by a veterinary specialist.

by both parents, who appear (phenotypically) normal but have a recessive gene for the disease, meaning that they carry, but are not affected by, the disease. These diseases pose serious problems to breeders because in some instances there are no methods of identifying carriers. Often the secondary diseases associated with these skin conditions are even more debilitating than the skin disorders themselves, including cancers and respiratory problems.

PARASITE BITES
Many of us are allergic to insect bites. The bites itch, erupt and may even become infected. Dogs have the same reaction to fleas, ticks and/or mites. When an insect lands on you, you have the chance to whisk it away with your

hand. Unfortunately, when a dog is bitten by a flea, tick or mite, it can only scratch it away or bite it. By the time the dog has been bitten, the parasite has done some of its damage. It may also have laid eggs, which will cause further problems in the near future. The itching from parasite bites is probably due to the saliva injected into the site when the parasite sucks the dog's blood.

AIRBORNE ALLERGIES

Just as humans suffer from hay fever during the pollinating season, many dogs suffer from the same allergies. When the pollen count is high, your dog might suffer, but don't expect him to sneeze and have a runny nose as a human would. Dogs react to pollen allergies in the same way they react to fleas—they scratch and bite themselves. Dogs, like humans, can be tested for allergens. Discuss the testing with your veterinary surgeon.

'P' STANDS FOR PROBLEM

Urinary tract disease is a serious condition that requires immediate medical attention. Symptoms include urinating in inappropriate places or the need to urinate frequently in small amounts. Urinary tract disease is most effectively treated with antibiotics. To help promote good urinary tract health, owners must always be sure that a constant supply of fresh water is available to their pets.

AUTO-IMMUNE ILLNESSES

An auto-immune illness is one in which the immune system overacts and does not recognise parts of the affected person; rather, the immune system starts to react as if these parts were foreign and need to be destroyed. An example is rheumatoid arthritis, which occurs when the body does not recognise the joints, thus leading to a very

DENTAL HEALTH

A dental examination is in order when the dog is between six months and one year of age so that any permanent teeth that have erupted incorrectly can be corrected. It is important to begin a brushing routine and follow through with this home dental plan for the life of your dog. Durable nylon and safe edible chews should be a part of your Sealy's arsenal for good health, good teeth and pleasant breath. The vast majority of dogs three to four years old and older has diseases of the gums from lack of dental attention. Using the various types of dental chews can be very effective in controlling dental plaque.

painful and damaging reaction in the joints. This has nothing to do with age, so can occur in children. The wear-and-tear arthritis of the older person or dog is osteoarthritis.

Lupus is an auto-immune disease that affects dogs as well as people. It can take variable forms, affecting the kidneys, bones and the skin. It can be fatal, so is treated with steroids, which can themselves have very significant side effects. The steroids calm down the allergic reaction to the body's tissues, which helps the lupus, but also calms down the body's reaction to real foreign substances such as bacteria, and also thins the skin and bone.

FOOD ALLERGIES

Dogs are allergic to many foods that are best-sellers and highly recommended by breeders and veterinary surgeons. Changing the brand of food that you buy may not eliminate the problem if the element to which the dog is allergic is contained in the new brand.

Recognising a food allergy can be difficult. Humans often have rashes when they eat foods to which they are allergic, or have swelling of the lips or eyes. Dogs do not usually develop rashes, but react in the same way as they do to an airborne or bite allergy— they itch, scratch and bite. While

CUSHING'S DISEASE
Cases of hyperactive adrenal glands (Cushing's disease) have been traced to the drinking of highly chlorinated water. Aerate or age your dog's drinking water before offering it.

pollen allergies and parasite bites are usually seasonal, pollen allergies are year-round problems.

TREATING FOOD ALLERGY

Diagnosis of food allergy is based on a two- to four-week dietary trial with an home-cooked diet fed to the exclusion of all other foods. The diet should consist of boiled rice or potato with a source of protein that the dog has never eaten before, such as fresh or frozen fish, lamb or even something as exotic as pheasant. Water has to be the only drink, and it is really important that no other foods are fed during this trial. If the dog's condition improves, you will need to try the original diet once again to see if the itching resumes. If it does, then this confirms the diagnosis that the dog is allergic to its original diet. The treatment is long-term feeding of something that does not distress the dog's skin, which may be in the form of one of the commercially available hypoallergenic diets or the home-made diet that you created for the allergy trial.

A male dog flea,
Ctenocephalides canis.

EXTERNAL PARASITES

FLEAS

Of all the problems to which dogs are prone, none is more well known and frustrating than fleas. Flea infestation is relatively simple to cure but difficult to prevent. Parasites that are harboured inside the body are a bit more difficult to eradicate but they are easier to control.

To control flea infestation, you have to understand the flea's life cycle. Fleas are often thought of as a summertime problem, but centrally heated homes have changed the patterns and fleas can be found at any time of the year.

The most effective method of flea control is a two-stage approach: one stage to kill the adult fleas, and the other to control the development of pre-adult fleas. Unfortunately, no single active ingredient is effective against all stages of the life cycle.

LIFE CYCLE STAGES

During its life, a flea will pass through four life stages: egg, larva, pupa and adult. The adult stage is the most visible and irritating stage of the flea life cycle, and this is why the majority of flea-control products concentrate on this stage. The fact is that adult fleas account for only 1% of the total flea population, and the other 99% exist in pre-adult stages, i.e. eggs, larvae and pupae. The pre-adult stages are barely visible to the naked eye.

THE LIFE CYCLE OF THE FLEA

Eggs are laid on the dog, usually in quantities of about 20 or 30, several times a day. The adult female flea must have a blood meal before each egg-laying session. When first laid, the eggs will cling to the dog's hair, as the eggs are still moist. However, they will quickly dry out and fall from the dog, especially if the dog moves around or scratches. Many eggs will fall off in the dog's favourite area or an area in which he spends a lot of time, such as his bed.

Once the eggs fall from the dog onto the carpet or furniture, they will hatch into larvae. This takes from one to ten days. Larvae are not particularly mobile and will usually travel only a few

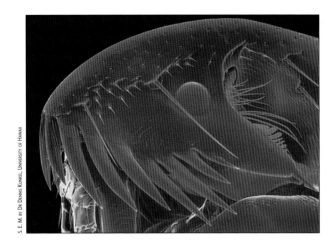

S.E.M. BY DR DENNIS KUNKEL, UNIVERSITY OF HAWAII

Magnified head of a dog flea, *Ctenocephalides canis*, colorized for effect.

inches from where they hatch. However, they do have a tendency to move away from light and heavy traffic—under furniture and behind doors are common places to find high quantities of flea larvae.

The flea larvae feed on dead organic matter, including adult flea faeces, until they are ready to change into adult fleas. Fleas will usually remain as larvae for around seven days. After this period, the larvae will pupate into protective pupae. While inside the pupae, the larvae will undergo metamorphosis and change into adult fleas. This can take as little time as a few days, but the adult fleas can remain inside the pupae waiting to hatch for up to two years. The pupae are signalled to hatch by certain stimuli, such as physical pressure—the pupae's being stepped on, heat from an animal's lying on the pupae or

FLEA KILLERS

Flea-killers are poisonous. You should not spray these toxic chemicals on areas of a dog's body that he licks, on his genitals or on his face. Flea killers taken internally are a better answer, but check with your vet in case internal therapy is not advised for your dog.

The dog flea is the most common parasite found on pet dogs.

S. E. M. by Dr Dennis Kunkel, University of Hawaii

increased carbon-dioxide levels and vibrations—indicating that a suitable host is available.

Once hatched, the adult flea must feed within a few days. Once the adult flea finds an host, it will not leave voluntarily. It only becomes dislodged by grooming or the host animal's scratching. The adult flea will remain on the host for the duration of its life unless forcibly removed.

Dwight R Kuhn's magnificent action photo, showing a flea jumping from a dog's back.

Photo by Dwight R Kuhn

TREATING THE ENVIRONMENT AND THE DOG

Treating fleas should be a two-pronged attack. First, the environment needs to be treated; this includes carpets and furniture, especially the dog's bedding and areas underneath furniture. The environment should be treated with an household spray containing an Insect Growth Regulator (IGR) and an insecticide to kill the adult fleas. Most IGRs are effective against eggs and larvae; they actually mimic the fleas' own hormones and stop the eggs and larvae from developing into adult fleas. There are currently no treatments available to attack the pupa stage of the life cycle, so the adult insecticide is used to kill the newly hatched adult fleas before they find an host. Most IGRs are active for many months, while adult insecticides are only active for a few days.

When treating with an household spray, it is a good idea to vacuum before applying the product. This stimulates as many pupae as possible to hatch into adult fleas. The vacuum cleaner should also be treated with an insecticide to prevent the eggs and larvae that have been hoovered into the vacuum bag from hatching.

The second stage of treatment is to apply an adult insecticide to

EN GARDE: CATCHING FLEAS OFF GUARD!

Consider the following ways to arm yourself against fleas:

- Add a small amount of pennyroyal or eucalyptus oil to your dog's bath. These natural remedies repel fleas.
- Supplement your dog's food with fresh garlic (minced or grated) and an hearty amount of brewer's yeast, both of which ward off fleas.
- Use a flea comb on your dog daily. Submerge fleas in a cup of bleach to kill them quickly.
- Confine the dog to only a few rooms to limit the spread of fleas in the home.
- Vacuum daily...and get all of the crevices! Dispose of the bag every few days until the problem is under control.
- Wash your dog's bedding daily. Cover cushions where your dog sleeps with towels, and wash the towels often.

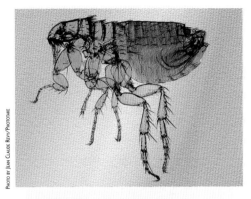

A LOOK AT FLEAS

Fleas have been around for millions of years and have adapted to changing host animals. They are able to go through a complete life cycle in less than one month or they can extend their lives to almost two years by remaining as pupae or cocoons. They do not need blood or any other food for up to 20 months.

They have been measured as being able to jump 300,000 times and can jump 150 times their length in any direction, including straight up. Those are just a few of the reasons why they are so successful in infesting a dog!

THE LIFE CYCLE OF THE FLEA

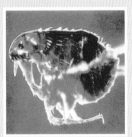

Eggs   **Larvae**   **Pupa**   **Adult**

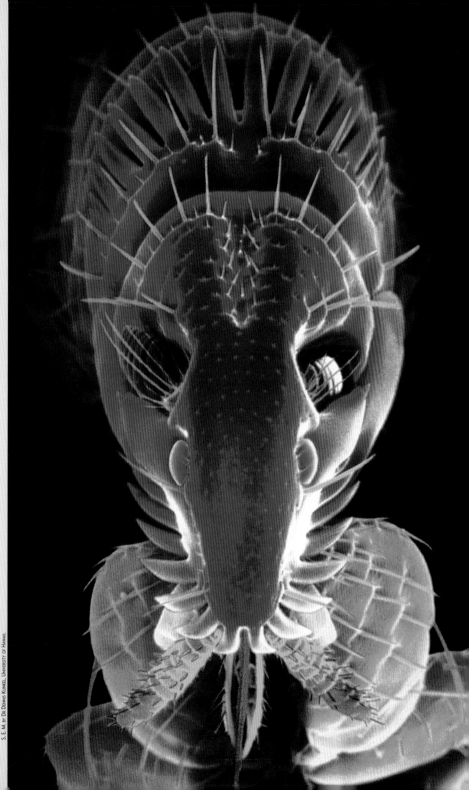

A scanning electron micrograph of a dog or cat flea, *Ctenocephalides,* magnified more than 100x. This image has been colorized for effect.

the dog. Traditionally, this would be in the form of a collar or a spray, but more recent innovations include digestible insecticides that poison the fleas when they ingest the dog's blood. Alternatively, there are drops that, when placed on the back of the animal's neck, spread throughout the fur and skin to kill adult fleas.

INSECT GROWTH REGULATOR (IGR)

Two types of products should be used when treating fleas—a product to treat the pet and a product to treat the home. Adult fleas represent less than 1% of the flea population. The pre-adult fleas (eggs, larvae and pupae) represent more than 99% of the flea population and are found in the environment; it is in the case of pre-adult fleas that products containing an Insect Growth Regulator (IGR) should be used in the home.

IGRs are a new class of compounds used to prevent the development of insects. They do not kill the insect outright, but instead use the insect's biology against it to stop it from completing its growth. Products that contain methoprene are the world's first and leading IGRs. Used to control fleas and other insects, this type of IGR will stop flea larvae from developing and protect the house for up to seven months.

A DEADLY MIX

Never mix flea control products without first consulting your vet. Some products can become toxic when combined with others and can cause fatal consequences.

TICKS AND MITES

Though not as common as fleas, ticks and mites are found all over the tropical and temperate world. They don't bite, like fleas; they harpoon. They dig their sharp proboscis (nose) into the dog's skin and drink the blood. Their only food and drink is dog's blood. Dogs can get Lyme disease, Rocky Mountain spotted fever (normally found in the US only), paralysis and many other diseases from ticks and mites. They may live where fleas are found and they like to hide in cracks or seams in walls wherever dogs live. They are controlled the same way fleas are controlled.

The dog tick, *Dermacentor variabilis*, may well be the most common dog tick in many geographical areas, especially those areas where the climate is hot and humid. Most dog ticks

A brown dog tick, *Rhipicephalus sanguineus*, is an uncommon but annoying tick found on dogs.

The head of a dog tick, *Dermacentor variabilis*, enlarged and colorized for effect.

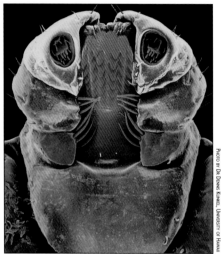

PHOTO BY DR. DENNIS KUNKEL, UNIVERSITY OF HAWAII

DEER-TICK CROSSING

The great outdoors may be fun for your dog, but it also is an home to dangerous ticks. Deer ticks carry a bacterium known as *Borrelia burgdorferi* and are most active in the autumn and spring. When infections are caught early, penicillin and tetracycline are effective antibiotics, but if left untreated the bacteria may cause neurological, kidney and cardiac problems as well as long-term trouble with walking and painful joints.

S. E. M. BY DR. ANDREW SPIELMAN/PHOTOTAKE.

have life expectancies of a week to six months, depending upon climatic conditions. They can neither jump nor fly, but they can crawl slowly and can range up to 5 metres (16 feet) to reach a sleeping or unsuspecting dog.

Human lice look like dog lice; the two are closely related.

PHOTO BY DWIGHT R KUHN

MANGE

Mites cause a skin irritation called mange. Some mites are contagious, like *Cheyletiella*, ear mites, scabies and chiggers. Mites that infest ears are usually controlled with Lindane,

which can only be administered by a vet, followed by Tresaderm at home. It is essential that your dog be treated for mange as quickly as possible because some forms of mange are transmissible to people.

Opposite page:
The dog tick, *Dermacentor variabilis*, is probably the most common tick found on dogs. Look at the strength in its eight legs! No wonder it's hard to detach them.

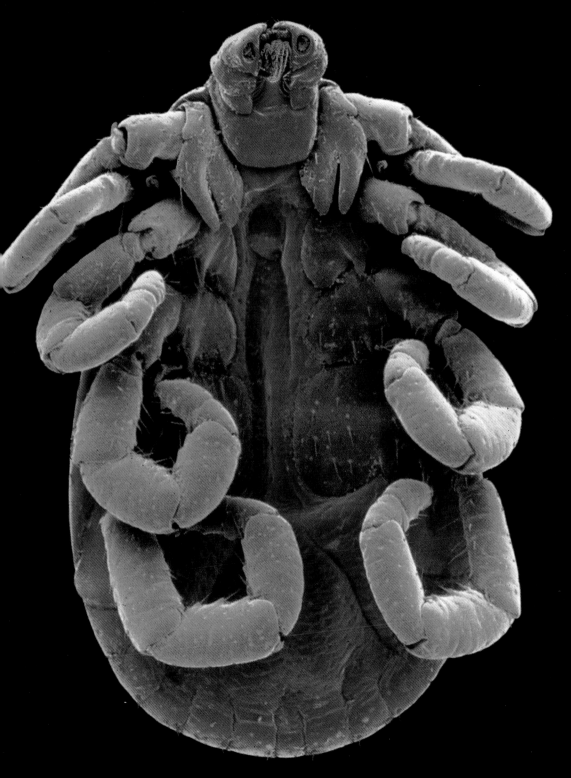

The mange mite, Psoroptes bovis.

INTERNAL PARASITES

Most animals—fishes, birds and mammals, including dogs and humans—have worms and other parasites that live inside their bodies. According to Dr Herbert R Axelrod, the fish pathologist, there are two kinds of parasites: dumb and smart. The smart parasites live in peaceful cooperation with their hosts (symbiosis), while the dumb parasites kill their hosts. Most of the worm infections are relatively easy to control. If they are not controlled, they weaken the host dog to the point that other medical problems occur, but they do not kill the host as dumb parasites would.

ROUNDWORMS

The roundworms that infect dogs are known scientifically as *Toxocara canis*. They live in the dog's intestines. The worms shed eggs continually. It has been estimated that a dog produces about 150 grammes of faeces every day. Each gramme of faeces averages 10,000–12,000 eggs of roundworms. There are no known areas in which dogs roam that do not contain roundworm eggs. The greatest danger of roundworms is

ROUNDWORMS

Average-size dogs can pass 1,360,000 roundworm eggs every day. For example, if there were only 1 million dogs in the world, the world would be saturated with 1,300 metric tonnes of dog faeces. These faeces would contain 15,000,000,000 roundworm eggs.

Up to 31% of home gardens and children's play boxes in the US contain roundworm eggs.

Flushing dog's faeces down the toilet is not a safe practice because the usual sewage treatments do not destroy roundworm eggs.

Infected puppies start shedding roundworm eggs at 3 weeks of age. They can be infected by their mother's milk.

The roundworm *Rhabditis* can infect both dogs and humans.

that they infect people too! It is wise to have your dog tested regularly for roundworms.

Pigs also have roundworm infections that can be passed to humans and dogs. The typical roundworm parasite is called *Ascaris lumbricoides*.

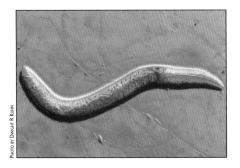

DEWORMING

Ridding your puppy of worms is *very important* because certain worms that puppies carry, such as tapeworms and roundworms, can infect humans.

Breeders initiate deworming programmes at or about four weeks of age. The routine is repeated every two or three weeks until the puppy is three months old. The breeder from whom you obtained your puppy should provide you with the complete details of the deworming programme.

Your veterinary surgeon can prescribe and monitor the programme of deworming for you. The usual programme is treating the puppy every 15–20 days until the puppy is positively worm-free. It is advised that you only treat your puppy with drugs that are recommended professionally.

The common roundworm, *Ascaris lumbricoides*.

Left: *Ancylostoma caninum* are uncommonly found in pet or show dogs in Britain.

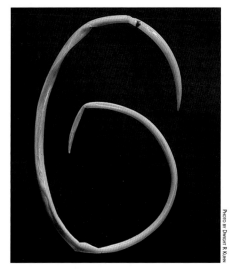

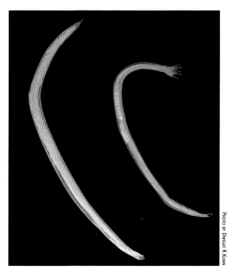

PHOTO BY DWIGHT R. KUHN

PHOTO BY DWIGHT R. KUHN

Right: Male and female hookworms.

HOOKWORMS

The worm *Ancylostoma caninum* is commonly called the dog hookworm. It is also dangerous to humans and cats. It has teeth by which it attaches itself to the intestines of the dog. It changes the site of its attachment about six times a day and the dog loses blood from each detachment, possibly causing iron-deficiency anaemia. Hookworms are easily purged from the dog with many medications. Milbemycin oxime, which also serves as an heartworm preventative in

The infective stage of the hookworm larva.

Collies, can be used for this purpose.

In Britain, the 'temperate climate' hookworm (*Uncinaria stenocephala*) is rarely found in pet or show dogs, but can occur in hunting packs, racing Greyhounds and sheepdogs because the worms can be prevalent wherever dogs are exercised regularly on grassland.

TAPEWORMS

There are many species of tapeworm, all of which are carried by fleas! The dog eats the flea and starts the tapeworm cycle. Humans can also be infected with tapeworms—so don't eat fleas! Fleas are so small that your dog could pass them onto your hands, your plate or your food and thus make it possible for you to ingest a flea that is carrying tapeworm eggs.

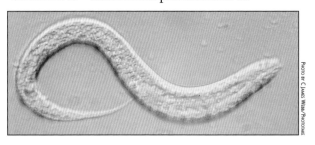

PHOTO BY C JAMES WEBB/PHOTOTAKE

TAPEWORMS

Humans, rats, squirrels, foxes, coyotes, wolves and domestic dogs are all susceptible to tapeworm infection. Except in humans, tapeworms are usually not a fatal infection. Infected individuals can harbour 1000 parasitic worms.

Tapeworms, like some other types of worm, are hermaphroditic, meaning male and female in the same worm.

If dogs eat infected rats or mice, they get the tapeworm disease. One month after attaching to a dog's intestine, the worm starts shedding eggs. These eggs are infective immediately. Infective eggs can live for a few months without an host animal.

While tapeworm infection is not life-threatening in dogs (smart parasite!), it can be the cause of a very serious liver disease for humans. About 50 percent of the humans infected with *Echinococcus multilocularis*, a type of tapeworm that causes alveolar hydatis, perish.

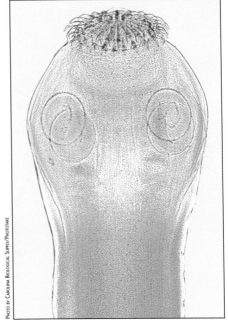

PHOTO BY CAROLINA BIOLOGICAL SUPPLY/PHOTOTAKE

The head and rostellum (the round prominence on the scolex) of a tapeworm, which infects dogs and humans.

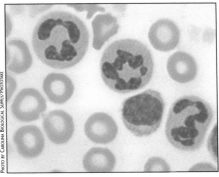

PHOTO BY CAROLINA BIOLOGICAL SUPPLY/PHOTOTAKE

Magnified heartworm larvae, *Dirofilaria immitis.*

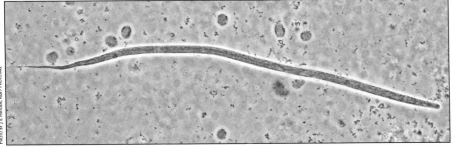

PHOTO BY J E HAYDON, RBP/PHOTOTAKE

Heartworm, *Dirofilaria immitis.*

First Aid at a Glance

Burns
Place the affected area under cool water; use ice if only a small area is burnt.

Insect bites
Apply ice to relieve swelling; antihistamine dosed properly.

Animal bites
Clean any bleeding area; apply pressure until bleeding subsides; go to the vet.

Spider bites
Use cold compress and a pressurised pack to inhibit venom's spreading.

Antifreeze poisoning
Induce vomiting with hydrogen peroxide. Seek *immediate* veterinary help!

Fish hooks
Removal best handled by vet; hook must be cut in order to remove.

Snake bites
Pack ice around bite; contact vet quickly; identify snake for proper antivenin.

Road-traffic accident
Move dog from roadway with blanket; seek veterinary aid.

Shock
Calm the dog, keep him warm; seek immediate veterinary help.

Nosebleed
Apply cold compress to the nose; apply pressure to any visible abrasion.

Bleeding
Apply pressure above the area; treat wound by applying a cotton pack.

Heat stroke
Submerge dog in cold bath; cool down with fresh air and water; go to the vet.

Frostbite/Hypothermia
Warm the dog with a warm bath, electric blankets or hot water bottles.

Abrasions
Clean the wound and wash out thoroughly with fresh water; apply antiseptic.

 Remember: an injured dog may attempt to bite an helping hand from fear and confusion. Always muzzle the dog before trying to offer assistance.

HEARTWORMS

Heartworms are thin, extended worms up to 30 cms (12 ins) long, which live in a dog's heart and the major blood vessels surrounding it. Dogs may have up to 200 worms. Symptoms may be loss of energy, loss of appetite, coughing, the development of a pot belly and anaemia.

Heartworms are transmitted by mosquitoes. The mosquito drinks the blood of an infected dog and takes in larvae with the blood. The larvae, called microfilaria, develop within the body of the mosquito and are passed on to the next dog bitten after the larvae mature. It takes two to three weeks for the larvae to develop to the infective stage within the body of the mosquito. Dogs should be treated at about six weeks of age, and maintained on a prophylactic dose given monthly.

Blood testing for heartworms is not necessarily indicative of how seriously your dog is infected. This is a dangerous disease. Although heartworm is a problem for dogs in America, Australia, Asia and Central Europe, dogs in the United Kingdom are not currently affected by heartworm.

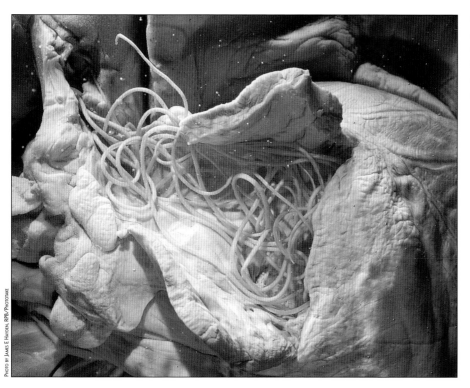

The heart of a dog infected with canine heartworm, *Dirofilaria immitis.*

HOMEOPATHY:
an alternative
to conventional
medicine

'Less is Most'

Using this principle, the strength of an homeopathic remedy is measured by the number of serial dilutions that were undertaken to create it. The greater the number of serial dilutions, the greater the strength of the homeopathic remedy. The potency of a remedy that has been made by making a dilution of 1 part in 100 parts (or 1/100) is 1c or 1cH. If this remedy is subjected to a series of further dilutions, each one being 1/100, a more dilute and stronger remedy is produced. If the remedy is diluted in this way six times, it is called 6c or 6cH. A dilution of 6c is 1 part in 1,000,000,000,000. In general, higher potencies in more frequent doses are better for acute symptoms and lower potencies in more infrequent doses are more useful for chronic, long-standing problems.

CURING OUR DOGS NATURALLY

Holistic medicine means treating the whole animal as a unique, perfect living being. Generally, holistic treatments do not suppress the symptoms that the body naturally produces, as do most medications prescribed by conventional doctors and vets. Holistic methods seek to cure disease by regaining balance and harmony in the patient's environment. Some of these methods include use of nutritional therapy, herbs, flower essences, aromatherapy, acupuncture, massage, chiropractic and, of course, the most popular holistic approach, homeopathy.

Homeopathy is a theory or system of treating illness with small doses of substances which, if administered in larger quantities, would produce the symptoms that the patient already has. This approach is often described as 'like cures like.' Although modern veterinary medicine is geared toward the 'quick fix,' homeopathy relies on the belief that, given the time, the body is able to heal itself and return to its natural, healthy state.

Choosing a remedy to cure a problem in our dogs is the difficult part of homeopathy. Consult with your veterinary surgeon for a professional diagnosis of your dog's symptoms. Often these symptoms require immediate conventional care. If your vet is willing and knowledgeable, you may attempt an homeopathic remedy. Be aware that cortisone prevents homeopathic remedies from working. There are hundreds of possibilities and combinations to cure many problems in dogs, from basic physical problems such as excessive moulting, fleas or other parasites, unattractive doggy odour, bad breath, upset tummy, obesity,

dry, oily or dull coat, diarrhoea, ear problems or eye discharge (including tears and dry or mucousy matter), to behavioural abnormalities such as fear of loud noises, habitual licking, poor appetite, excessive barking and various phobias. From alumina to zincum metallicum, the remedies span the planet and the imagination…from flowers and weeds to chemicals, insect droppings, diesel smoke and volcanic ash.

Using 'Like to Treat Like'

Unlike conventional medicines that suppress symptoms, homeopathic remedies treat illnesses with small doses of substances that, if administered in larger quantities, would produce the symptoms that the patient already has. While the same homeopathic remedy can be used to treat different symptoms in different dogs, here are some interesting remedies and their uses.

Apis Mellifica
(made from honey bee venom) can be used for allergies or to reduce swelling that occurs in acutely infected kidneys.

Diesel Smoke
can be used to help control travel sickness.

Calcarea Fluorica
(made from calcium fluoride, which helps harden bone structure) can be useful in treating hard lumps in tissues.

Natrum Muriaticum
(made from common salt, sodium chloride) is useful in treating thin, thirsty dogs.

Nitricum Acidum
(made from nitric acid) is used for symptoms you would expect to see from contact with acids, such as lesions, especially where the skin joins the linings of body orifices or openings such as the lips and nostrils.

Symphytum
(made from the herb Knitbone, *Symphytum officianale*) is used to encourage bones to heal.

Urtica Urens
(made from the common stinging nettle) is used in treating painful, irritating rashes.

Owners and
breeders look for
Sealyham Terriers
with clear,
healthy eyes.

Owners and breeders look for Sealyham Terriers with clear, healthy eyes.

A PET OWNER'S GUIDE TO COMMON OPHTHALMIC DISEASES
by Prof. Dr Robert L Peiffer, Jr

Few would argue that vision is the most important of the cognitive senses, and maintenance of a normal visual system is important for an optimal quality of life. Likewise, pet owners tend to be acutely aware of their pet's eyes and vision, which is important because early detection of ocular disease will optimise therapeutic outcomes. The eye is a sensitive organ with minimal reparative capabilities, and with some diseases, such as glaucoma, uveitis and retinal detachment, delay in diagnosis and treatment can be critical in terms of whether vision can be preserved.

Lower entropion, or rolling in of the eyelid, is causing irritation in the left eye of this young dog. Several extra eyelashes, or distichiasis, are present on the upper lid.

The causes of ocular disease are quite varied; the nature of dogs makes them susceptible to traumatic conditions, the most common of which include proptosis of the globe, cat scratch injuries and penetrating wounds

from foreign objects, including sticks and air rifle pellets. Infectious diseases caused by bacteria, viruses or fungi may be localised to the eye or part of a systemic infection. Many of the common conditions, including eyelid conformational problems, cataracts, glaucoma and retinal degenerations, have a genetic basis.

Before acquiring your puppy, it is important to ascertain that both parents have been examined and certified free of eye disease by a veterinary ophthalmologist. Since many of these genetic diseases can be detected early in life, acquire the pup with the condition that it pass a thorough ophthalmic examination by a qualified specialist.

LID CONFORMATIONAL ABNORMALITIES

Rolling in (entropion) or out (ectropion) of the lids tends to be a breed-related problem. Entropion can involve the upper and/or lower lids. Signs usually appear between 3 and 12 months of age. The irritation caused by the eyelid hairs' rubbing

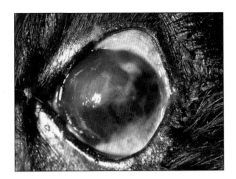

on the surface of the cornea may result in blinking, tearing and damage to the cornea.

Ectropion is likewise breed-related and is considered 'normal' in hounds, for instance; unlike entropion, which results in acute discomfort, ectropion may cause chronic irritation related to exposure and the pooling of secretions. Most of these cases can be managed medically with daily irrigation with sterile saline and topical antibiotics when required.

Eyelash Abnormalities

Dogs normally have lashes only on the upper lids, in contrast to humans. Occasionally, extra eyelashes may be seen emerging at the eyelid margin (distichiasis) or through the inner surface of the eyelid (ectopic cilia).

Conjunctivitis

Inflammation of the conjunctiva, the pink tissue that lines the lids and the anterior portion of the sclera, is generally accompanied by redness, discharge and mild discomfort. The majority of cases are either associated with bacterial infections or dry-eye syndrome. Fortunately, topical medications are generally effective in curing or controlling the problem.

Dry Eye Syndrome

Dry eye syndrome (keratoconjunctivitis sicca) is a common cause of external ocular disease. Discharge is typically thick and sticky, and keratitis is a frequent component; any breed can be affected. While some cases can be associated with the toxic effects of drugs, including the sulfa antibiotics, the cause in the majority of the cases cannot be determined and is assumed to be immune-mediated.

Keratoconjunctivitis sicca, seen here in the right eye of a middle-aged dog, causes a characteristic thick mucous discharge as well as secondary corneal changes.

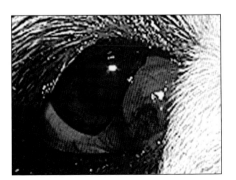

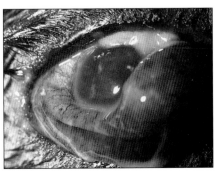

Left: Prolapse of the gland of the third eyelid in the right eye of a pup. Right: In this case, in the right eye of a young dog, the prolapsed gland can be seen emerging between the edge of the third eyelid and the corneal surface.

Multiple deep ulcerations affect the cornea of this middle-aged dog.

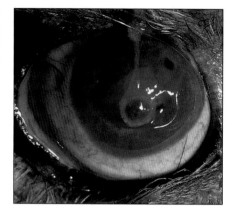

PROLAPSE OF THE GLAND OF THE THIRD EYELID

In this condition, commonly referred to as *cherry eye*, the gland of the third eyelid, which produces about one-third of the aqueous phase of the tear film and is normally situated within the anterior orbit, prolapses to emerge as a pink fleshy mass protruding over the edge of the third eyelid, between the third eyelid and the cornea. The condition usually develops during the first year of life and, while mild irritation may result, the condition is unsightly as much as anything else.

Lipid deposition can occur as a primary inherited dystrophy, or secondarily to hypercholesterolemia (in dogs, frequently associated with hypothyroidism), chronic corneal inflammation or neoplasia. The deposits in this dog assume an oval pattern in the centre of the cornea.

CORNEAL DISEASE

The cornea is the clear front part of the eye that provides the first step in the collection of light on its journey eventually to be focused onto the retina, and most corneal diseases will be manifested by alterations in corneal transparency. The cornea is an exquisitely innervated tissue, and defects in corneal integrity are accompanied by pain, which is demonstrated by squinting.

Corneal ulcers may occur secondarily to trauma or to irritation from entropion or ectopic cilia. In middle-aged or older dogs, epithelial ulcerations may occur spontaneously due to an inherent defect; these are referred to as indolent or Boxer ulcers, in recognition of the breed in which we see the condition most frequently. Infection may occur secondarily. Ulcers can be potentially blinding conditions; severity is dependent upon the size and depth of the ulcer and other complicating features.

Non-ulcerative keratitis tends to have an immune-mediated component and is managed by topical immunosuppressants, usually corticosteroids. Corneal edema can occur in elderly dogs. It is due to a failure of the corneal endothelial 'pump.'

The cornea responds to chronic irritation by transforming

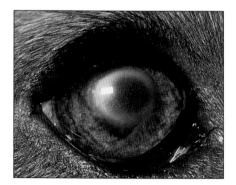

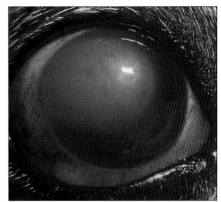

into skin-like tissue that is evident clinically by pigmentation, scarring and vascularisation; some cases may respond to tear stimulants, lubricants and topical corticosteroids, while others benefit from surgical narrowing of the eyelid opening in order to enhance corneal protection.

UVEITIS

Inflammation of the vascular tissue of the eye—the uvea—is a common and potentially serious disease in dogs. While it may occur secondarily to trauma or other intraocular diseases, such as cataracts, most

commonly uveitis is associated with some type of systemic infectious or neoplastic process. Uncontrolled, uveitis can lead to blinding cataracts, glaucoma and/or retinal detachments, and aggressive symptomatic therapy with dilating agents (to prevent pupillary adhesions) and anti-inflammatories are critical.

GLAUCOMA

The eye is essentially an hollow fluid-filled sphere, and the pressure within is maintained by regulation of the rate of fluid production and fluid egress at 10–20 mms of mercury. The retinal cells are extremely sensitive to elevations of intraocular pressure and, unless controlled, permanent blindness can occur within hours to days. In acute glaucoma, the conjunctiva becomes congested, the cornea cloudy, the pupil moderate and fixed; the eye is generally painful and avisual. Increased constant signs of

Corneal edema can develop as a slowly progressive process in Sealys and many other breeds, as a result of the inability of the corneal endothelial pump to maintain a state of dehydration.

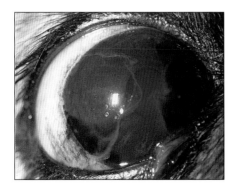

Medial pigmentary keratitis in this dog is associated with irritation from prominent facial folds.

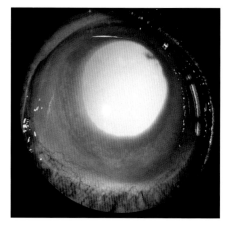

Glaucoma in the dog most commonly occurs as a sudden extreme elevation of intraocular pressure, frequently to three to four times the norm. The eye of this dog demonstrates the common signs of episcleral injection, or redness; mild diffuse corneal cloudiness, due to edema; and a mid-sized fixed pupil.

discomfort will accompany chronic cases.

Management of glaucoma is one of the most challenging situations the veterinary ophthalmologist faces; in spite of intense efforts, many of these cases will result in blindness.

CATARACTS AND LENS DISLOCATION

Cataracts are the most common blinding condition in dogs; fortunately, they are readily amenable to surgical intervention, with excellent results in terms of restoration of vision and replace-

ment of the cataractous lens with a synthetic one. Most cataracts in dogs are inherited; less commonly, cataracts can be secondary to trauma, other ocular diseases, including uveitis, glaucoma, lens luxation and retinal degeneration, or secondary to an underlying systemic metabolic disease, including diabetes and Cushing's disease. Signs include a progressive loss of the bright dark appearance of the pupil, which is replaced by a blue-grey hazy appearance. In this respect, cataracts need to be distinguished from the normal ageing process of nuclear sclerosis, which occurs in middle-aged or older animals, and has minimal effect on vision.

Lens dislocation occurs in dogs and frequently leads to secondary glaucoma; early removal of the dislocated lens is generally curative.

RETINAL DISEASE

Retinal degenerations are usually inherited, but may be associated

Left: The typical posterior subcapsular cataract appears between one and two years of age, but rarely progresses to where the animal has visual problems. Right: Inherited cataracts generally appear between three and six years of age, and progress to the stage seen where functional vision is significantly impaired.

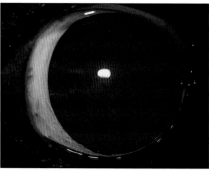

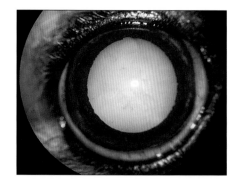

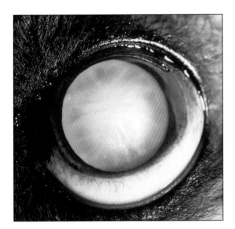

with vitamin E deficiency in dogs. While signs are variable, most frequently one notes a decrease in vision over a period of months, which typically starts out as night blindness. The cause of a more rapid loss of vision due to retinal degeneration occurs over days to weeks is labelled sudden acquired retinal degeneration or SARD; the outcome, however, is unfortunately usually similar to inherited and nutritional conditions, as the retinal tissues possess minimal regenerative capabilities. Most pets, however, with a bit of extra care and attention, show an amazing ability to adapt to an avisual world, and can be maintained as pets with a satisfactory quality of life.

Detachment of the retina—due to accumulation of blood between the retina and the underling uvea, which is called the *choroid*—can occur secondarily to retinal tears or holes, tractional forces within the eye, or as a result of uveitis. These types of detachments may be amenable to surgical repair if diagnosed early.

OPTIC NEURITIS

Optic neuritis, or inflammation of the nerve that connects the eye with the brain stem, is a relatively uncommon condition that presents usually with rather sudden loss of vision and widely dilated non-responsive pupils.

Anterior lens luxation can occur as a primary disease in the terrier breeds, or secondarily to trauma. The fibres that hold the lens in place rupture and the lens may migrate through the pupil to be situated in front of the iris. Secondary glaucoma is a frequent and significant complication that can be avoided if the dislocated lens is removed surgically.

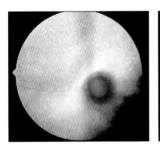
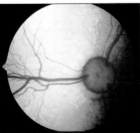
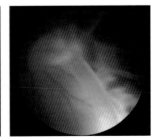

Left: The posterior pole of a normal fundus is shown; prominent are the head of the optic nerve and the retinal blood vessels. The retina is transparent, and the prominent green tapetum is seen superiorly.
Centre: An eye with inherited retinal dysplasia is depicted. The tapetal retina superior to the optic disc is disorganised, with multifocal areas of hyperplasia of the retinal pigment epithelium.
Right: Severe collie eye anomaly and a retinal detachment; this eye is unfortunately blind.

Behaviour of Your
SEALYHAM TERRIER

As an owner of a Sealyham Terrier, you have selected your dog so that you and your loved ones can have a companion, a protector, a friend and a four-legged family member. You invest time, money and effort to care for and train the family's new charge. Of course, this chosen canine behaves perfectly! Well, perfectly like a *dog*.

THINK LIKE A DOG

Dogs do not think like humans, nor do humans think like dogs, though we try. Unfortunately, a dog is incapable of compre-hending how humans think, so the responsibility falls on the owner to adopt a proper canine mindset. Dogs cannot rationalise, and dogs exist in the present moment. Many dog owners make the mistake in training of thinking that they can reprimand their dog for something he did a while ago. Basically, you cannot even reprimand a dog for something he did 20 seconds ago! Either catch him in the act or forget it! It is a waste of your and your dog's time—in his mind, you are reprimanding him for whatever he is doing at that moment.

The following behavioural problems represent some which owners most commonly encounter. Every dog is unique and every situation is unique. No author could purport for you to solve your Sealyham's problems simply by reading a script. Here we outline some basic 'dogspeak' so that owners' chances of solving behavioural problems are increased.

Discuss your Sealy's bad habits with your veterinary surgeon and he can recommend a behavioural specialist to consult in appropriate cases. Since behavioural abnormalities are the main reason for owners' abandoning their pets, we hope that you will make a valiant effort to solve your Sealyham's problems. Patience and understanding are virtues that must dwell in every pet-loving household.

AGGRESSION

This is a problem that concerns all responsible dog owners. Aggression can be a very big problem in dogs, and, when not controlled, always becomes dangerous. An aggressive dog—no matter the size—may lunge at, bite or even attack a person or another dog. Aggressive behaviour is not to be tolerated. It is more than just inappropriate behaviour; it is painful for a family to watch their dog become unpredictable in his behaviour to the point where they are afraid of him. While not all aggressive behaviour is dangerous, growling, baring teeth, etc. can be frightening. It is important to ascertain why the dog is acting in this manner. Aggression is a display of dominance, and the dog should not have the dominant role in its pack, which is, in this case, your family.

It is important not to challenge an aggressive dog, as this could provoke an attack. Observe your Sealyham's body language. Does he make direct eye contact and stare? Does he try to make himself as large as possible: ears pricked, chest out, tail erect? Height and size signify authority in a dog pack—being taller or 'above' another dog literally means that he is 'above' in social status. These body signals tell you that your Sealyham thinks he is in charge, a problem that needs to be addressed. An aggressive dog is unpredictable; you never know when he is going to strike and what he is going to do. You cannot understand why a dog that is playful one minute is growling the next.

Fear is a common cause of aggression in dogs. Perhaps your Sealyham had a negative experience as a puppy, which causes him to be fearful when a similar situation presents itself later in life. The dog may act aggressively in order to protect himself from whatever is making him afraid. It is not always easy to determine what is making your dog fearful, but if you can isolate what brings out the fear reaction, you can help the dog get over it.

Supervise your Sealyham's interactions with people and other dogs, and praise the dog when it goes well. If he starts to act aggressively in a situation, correct him and remove him from the

AIN'T MISBEHAVIN'
Punishment is rarely necessary for a misbehaving dog. Dogs that habitually behave badly probably had a poor education and do not know what is expected of them. They need training. Negative reinforcement on your part usually does more harm than good.

situation. Do not let people approach the dog and start petting him without your express permission. That way, you can have the dog sit to accept petting, and praise him when he behaves properly. You are focusing on praise and on modifying his behaviour by rewarding him when he acts appropriately. By being gentle and by supervising his interactions, you are showing him that there is no need to be afraid or defensive.

The best solution is to consult

Engaged in play, these two Sealyhams have a well-established rapport. Aggressive behaviour rarely arises between dogs who have a clear understanding of the rules of the pack.

a behavioural specialist, one who has experience with the Sealyham or other terrier breeders if possible. Together, perhaps you can pinpoint the cause of your dog's aggression and do something about it. An aggressive dog cannot be trusted, and a dog that cannot be trusted is not safe to have as a family pet. If, very unusually, you find that your pet has become untrustworthy and you feel it necessary to seek a new home with a more suitable family and environment, explain fully to the new owners all your reasons for rehoming the dog to be fair to all concerned. In the very worst case, you will have to consider euthanasia.

AGGRESSION TOWARD OTHER DOGS

A dog's aggressive behaviour toward another dog stems from not enough exposure to other dogs at an early age. If other dogs make your Sealyham nervous and agitated, he will lash out as a protective mechanism. A dog that has not received sufficient exposure to other canines tends to think that he is the only dog on the planet. The animal becomes so dominant that he does not even show signs that he is fearful or threatened. Without growling or any other physical signal as a warning, he will lunge at and bite the other dog.

A way to correct this is to let your Sealyham approach another dog when walking on lead. Watch very closely and, at the first sign of aggression, correct your Sealyham and pull him away. Scold him for any sign of discomfort, and then praise him when he ignores the other dog. Keep this up until either he stops the aggressive behaviour, learns to

---

SOUND BITES

When a dog bites, there is always a good reason for his doing so. Many dogs are trained to protect a person, an area or an object. When that person, area or object is violated, the dog will attack. A dog attacks with his mouth. He has no other means of attack.

Fighting dogs (and there are many breeds which fight) are taught to fight, but they also have a natural instinct to fight. This instinct is normally reserved for other dogs, though unfortunate accidents can occur; for example, when a baby crawls toward a fighting dog and the dog mistakes the crawling child as a potential attacker.

If a dog is a biter for seemingly no reason, if he bites the hand that feeds him or if he snaps at members of your family, see your veterinary surgeon or behaviourist immediately to learn how to modify the dog's behaviour.

ignore other dogs or even accepts other dogs. Praise him lavishly for this correct behaviour.

DOMINANT AGGRESSION

A social hierarchy is firmly established in a wild dog pack. The dog wants to dominate those under him and please those above him. Dogs know that there must be a leader. If you are not the obvious choice for emperor, the dog will assume the throne! These conflicting innate desires are what a dog owner is up against when he sets about training a dog. In training a dog to obey commands, the owner is reinforcing that he is the top dog in the 'pack' and that the dog should, and should want to, serve his superior. Thus, the owner is suppressing the dog's urge to dominate by modifying his behaviour and making him obedient.

An important part of training is taking every opportunity to reinforce that you are the leader. The simple action of making your Sealyham sit to wait for his food instead of allowing him to run up to get it when he wants it says that you control when he eats; he is dependent on you for food. Although it may be difficult, do not give in to your dog's wishes every time he whines or looks at you with pleading eyes. It is a constant effort to show the dog that his place in the pack is at the bottom.

FEAR IN A GROWN DOG

Fear in a grown dog is often the result of improper or incomplete socialisation as a pup, or it can be the result of a traumatic experience he suffered when young. Keep in mind that the term 'traumatic' is relative—something that you would not think twice about can leave a lasting negative impression on a puppy. If the dog experiences a similar experience later in life, he may try to fight back to protect himself. Again, this behaviour is very unpredictable, especially if you do not know what is triggering his fear.

This is not meant to sound cruel or inhumane. You love your Sealyham and you should treat him with care and affection. You (hopefully) did not get a dog just so you could control another creature. Dog training is not about being cruel or feeling important, it is about moulding the dog's behaviour into what is acceptable and teaching him to live by your

TUG-OF-WAR

You should never play tug-of-war games with your puppy. Such games create a struggle for 'top dog' position and teach the puppy that it is acceptable to challenge you. It will also encourage your puppy's natural tendency to bite down hard and *win*.

rules. In theory, it is quite simple: catch him in appropriate behaviour and reward him for it. Add a dog into the equation and it becomes a bit more trying, but as a rule of thumb, positive reinforcement is what works best.

With a dominant dog, punishment and negative reinforcement can have the opposite effect of what you are after. It can make a dog fearful and/or act out aggressively if he feels he is being challenged. Remember, a dominant dog perceives himself at the top of the social heap, and will fight to defend his perceived status. The best way to prevent that is to never give him reason to think that he is in control in the first place.

If you are having trouble training your Sealyham and it seems as if he is constantly challenging your authority, seek the help of an obedience trainer or behavioural specialist. A professional will work with both you and your dog to teach you effective techniques to use at home. Beware of trainers who rely on excessively harsh methods; scolding is necessary now and then, but the focus in your training should *always* be on positive reinforcement.

DIGGING
Digging, which is seen as a destructive behaviour to humans, is actually quite a natural behaviour in dogs, especially in terriers, who were bred to do just that—DIG! The 'earth dogs' are most associated with digging and are most inclined to 'go to ground.' When digging occurs in your garden, it is actually a normal behaviour redirected into something the dog can do in his

The Sealyham is an accomplished earthdog, for whom digging is a natural talent. If your Sealy insists upon rearranging your landscape, provide him with a place where he can practise his excavation techniques.

everyday life. In the wild, a dog would be actively seeking food, making his own shelter, etc. He would be using his paws in a purposeful manner for his survival. Since you provide him with food and shelter, he has no need to use his paws for these purposes, and so the energy that he would be using may manifest itself in the form of little holes all over your garden and flower beds.

Sealys bore easily, just as easily as they bore holes in your garden. Perhaps your Sealyham is digging as a reaction to simple boredom! The obvious answer is to provide the dog with adequate play and exercise so that his mind and paws are occupied, and so that he feels as if he is doing something useful. Exercise and toys are two of the most common

DOMINANT AGGRESSION
Never allow your puppy to growl at you or bare his tiny teeth. Such behaviour is dominant and aggressive. If not corrected, the dog will repeat the behaviour, which will become more threatening as he grows larger and will eventually lead to biting.

cures, and a second dog is a more extreme solution (but one worth considering).

Of course, digging is easiest to control if it is stopped as soon as possible, but it is often hard to catch a dog in the act. If your dog is a compulsive digger and is not easily distracted by other activities, you can designate an area on your property where he is allowed

Nipping at your trousers and shoes should be discouraged immediately. You must be in control of your whole Sealyham, including his mischief-seeking mouth.

This Sealyham urchin is practising his 'death grip' on a recalcitrant stuffed foe.

to dig. If you catch him digging in an off-limits area of the garden, immediately bring him to the approved area and praise him for digging there. Keep a close eye on him so that you can catch him in the act—that is the only way to make him understand what is permitted and what is not. If you take him to an hole he dug an hour ago and tell him 'No,' he will understand that you are not fond of holes, or dirt or flowers. If you catch him while he is stifle-deep in your tulips, that is when he will get your message.

CHEWING

The national canine pastime is chewing! Every dog loves to sink his 'canines' into a tasty bone, but, if a bone is not available, he'll sink his teeth into whatever he can. Dogs need to chew, to massage their gums, to make their new teeth feel better and to exercise their jaws. This is a natural behaviour that is deeply embedded in all things canine. Our role as owners is not to stop the dog's chewing, but rather to redirect it to positive, chew-worthy objects. Be an informed owner and purchase proper chew toys, like strong nylon bones, that will not splinter. Be sure that the objects are safe and durable, since your dog's safety is at risk. Again, the owner is responsible for ensuring a dog-proof environment.

The best answer is prevention; that is, put your shoes, handbags and other tasty objects in their proper places (out of the reach of the growing canine mouth). Direct puppies to their toys whenever you see them 'tasting' the furniture legs or the leg of your trousers. Make a loud noise to attract the pup's attention and immediately escort him to his chew toy and engage him with the toy for at least four minutes, praising and encouraging him all the while. An array of safe, interesting chew toys will keep your dog's mind and teeth occupied, and distracted from chewing on things he shouldn't.

Some trainers recommend deterrents, such as hot pepper, a bitter spice or a product designed for this purpose, to discourage the dog from chewing unwanted objects. Test these products to see which works best before investing in large quantities.

JUMPING UP

Jumping up is a dog's friendly way of saying hello! Some dog owners do not mind when their dog jumps up. The problem arises when guests come to the house and the dog greets them in the same manner—whether they like it or not! However friendly the greeting may be, the chances are that your visitors will not appreciate your dog's enthusiasm. The dog will not be able to distinguish upon whom he can jump and whom he cannot. Therefore, it is probably best to discourage this behaviour entirely.

Pick a command such as 'Off' (avoid using 'Down' since you will use that for the dog to lie down) and tell him 'Off' when he jumps up. Place him on the

> **NO JUMPING**
> Stop a dog from jumping up before he jumps. If he is getting ready to jump onto you, simply walk away. If he jumps up on you before you can turn away, lower his front paws to the ground while telling him 'Off.' Do not be forceful. Your dog soon will realise that jumping up is not a productive way of getting attention.

ground on all fours and have him sit, praising him the whole time. Always lavish him with praise and petting when he is in the sit position. In this way, you can give him a warm affectionate greeting, let him know that you are as excited to see him as he is to see you and instil good manners at the same time!

BARKING

Dogs cannot talk—oh, what they would say if they could! Instead,

> **BARKING STANCE**
> Did you know that a dog is less likely to bark when sitting than standing? Watch your dog the next time that you suspect he is about to start barking. You'll notice that as he does, he gets up on all four feet. Hence, when teaching a dog to stop barking, it helps to get him to sit before you command him to be quiet.

barking is a dog's way of 'talking.' It can be somewhat frustrating because it is not always easy to tell what a dog means by his bark—is he excited, happy, frightened or angry? Whatever it is that the dog is trying to say, he should not be punished for barking. It is only when the barking becomes excessive, and when the excessive barking becomes a bad habit, that the behaviour needs to be modified.

DOG TALK

Deciphering your dog's barks is very similar to understanding a baby's cries: there is a different cry for eating, sleeping, toilet needs, etc. Your dog talks to you not only through howls and groans but also through his body language. Baring teeth, staring and inflating the chest are all threatening gestures. If a dog greets you by licking his nose, turning his head or yawning, these are friendly, peacemaking gestures.

Fortunately, Sealyhams are not as vocal as most other dogs; they tend to use their barks more purposefully. If an intruder came into your home in the middle of the night and your Sealyham barked a warning, wouldn't you be pleased? You would probably deem your dog an hero, a wonderful guardian and protector of the home. On the other hand, if a friend drops by unexpectedly, rings the doorbell and is greeted with a sudden sharp bark, you would probably be annoyed at the dog. But in reality, isn't this just the same behaviour? The dog does not know any better. Unless he sees who is at the door and it is someone he knows, he will bark as a means of vocalising that his (and your) territory is being threatened. While your friend is not posing a threat, it is all the same to the dog. Barking is his means of letting you know that there is an intrusion, whether friend or foe, on your property. This type of barking is instinctive and should not be discouraged.

Excessive habitual barking, however, is a problem that should be corrected early on. As your Sealyham grows up, you will be able to tell when his barking is purposeful and when it is for no reason. You will become able to distinguish your dog's different barks and their meanings. For example, the bark when someone comes to the door will be different from the bark when he is excited to see you. It is similar to a person's tone of voice, except that the dog has to rely totally on tone of voice because he does not have the benefit of using words. An incessant barker will be evident at an early age.

There are some things that encourage a dog to bark. For example, if your dog barks nonstop for a few minutes and you give him a treat to quieten him, he believes that you are rewarding him for barking. He will associate barking with getting a treat and will keep doing it until he is rewarded. On the other hand, if you give him a command such as 'Quiet' and praise him after he has stopped barking for a few seconds, he will get the idea that being 'quiet' is what you want him to do.

SEPARATION ANXIETY

Recognised by behaviourists as the most common form of stress for dogs, separation anxiety can also lead to destructive behaviours in your dog. It's more than your Sealyham's howling his displeasure at your leaving the house and his being left alone. This is a normal reaction, no different from the child who cries as his mother leaves him on the first day at school. However, separation anxiety is more serious. In fact, if you are constantly with your dog, he will come to expect you with him all of the time, making it even more traumatic for him when you are not there.

One thing you can do to minimise separation anxiety is to make your entrances and exits as low-key as possible. Do not give your dog a long drawn-out goodbye, and do not lavish him with hugs and kisses when you

return. This is giving in to the attention that he craves, and it will only make him miss it more when you are away. Another thing you can try is to give your dog a treat when you leave; this will not only keep him occupied and keep his mind off the fact that you have just left, but it will also help him associate your leaving with a pleasant experience.

You may have to accustom your dog to being left alone at intervals. Of course, when your dog starts whimpering as you approach the door, your first instinct will be to run to him and comfort him, but do not do it! Eventually he will adjust to your absence. His anxiety stems from being placed in an unfamiliar situation; by familiarising him with being alone, he will learn that he will survive. That is not to say you should purposely leave

AGE OF ANXIETY
The number of dogs that suffer from separation anxiety is on the rise as more and more pet owners find themselves at work all day. New attention is being paid to this problem, which is especially hard to diagnose since it is only evident when the dog is alone. Research is currently being done to help educate dog owners about separation anxiety and how they can help minimise this problem in their dogs.

NO BUTTS ABOUT IT

Dogs get to know each other by sniffing each other's backsides. It seems that each dog has a telltale odour, probably created by the anal glands. It also distinguishes sex and signals when a female will be receptive to a male's attention. Some dogs snap at another dog's intrusion of their private parts.

your dog home alone, but the dog needs to know that, while he can depend on you for his care, you do not have to be by his side 24 hours a day. Some behaviourists recommend tiring the dog out before you leave home—take him for a good long walk or engage in a game of fetch in the garden.

SEXUAL BEHAVIOUR

Dogs exhibit certain sexual behaviours that may have influenced your choice of male or female when you first purchased your Sealyham. To a certain extent, spaying/neutering will eliminate these behaviours, but if you are purchasing a dog that you wish to breed from, you should be aware of what you will have to deal with throughout the dog's life.

Female dogs usually have two oestruses per year, with each season lasting about three weeks. These are the only times that a female dog will mate, and she usually will not allow this until the second week of the cycle, although this varies from bitch to bitch. If not bred during the heat cycle, it is not uncommon for a bitch to experience a false pregnancy, in which her mammary glands swell and she exhibits maternal tendencies toward toys or other objects.

With male dogs, owners must be aware that whole dogs (dogs who are not neutered) have the natural inclination to mark their territory. Males mark their territory by spraying small amounts of urine as they lift their legs in a macho ritual. Marking can occur both outdoors in the garden and around the neighbour-hood as well as indoors on furniture legs, curtains and the sofa. Such behaviour can be very frustrating for the owner; early training is strongly urged before the 'urge' strikes your dog. Neutering the male at an appropriate early age can solve this problem before it becomes an habit.

Other problems associated with males are wandering and mounting. Both of these habits, of course, belong to the unneutered dog, whose sexual drive leads him away from home in search of the bitch in heat. Males will mount females in heat, as well as any other dog, male or female, that happens to catch their fancy. Other possible mounting partners

Stealing food is not a crime in the eyes of a Sealy. Food left about is fair game as far as any dog is concerned.

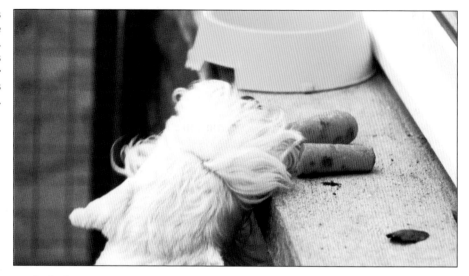

include his owner, the furniture, guests to the home and strangers on the street. Discourage such behaviour early on.

Owners must further recognise that mounting is not merely a sexual expression but also one of dominance. Be consistent and be persistent, and you will find that you can 'move mounters.'

FOOD STEALING

Is your dog devising ways of stealing food from your coffee table or kitchen counter? If so, you must answer the following questions: Is your Sealyham a bit peckish, or is he 'constantly famished' like many dogs seem to be? Face it, some dogs are more food-motivated than others. They are totally obsessed by the smell of food and can only think of their next meal. Food stealing is terrific

fun and always yields a great reward—FOOD, glorious food.

Your goal as an owner, therefore, is to be sensible about where food is placed in the home and to reprimand your dog whenever he is caught in the act of stealing. But remember, only reprimand your dog if you actually see him stealing, not later when the crime is discovered; that will be of no use at all and will only serve to confuse him.

BEGGING

Just like food stealing, begging is a favourite pastime of peckish puppies! It achieves that same lovely result—FOOD! Dogs quickly learn that their owners keep the 'good food' for ourselves, and that we humans do not dine on dried food alone. Begging is a conditioned response related to a specific stimulus, time and place. The sounds of the kitchen, cans and bottles opening, crinkling bags, the smell of food in preparation, etc., will excite the dog, and soon the paws will be in the air!

Here is the solution to stopping this behaviour: Never give in to a beggar! You are rewarding the dog for sitting pretty, jumping up, whining and rubbing his nose into you by giving him food. By ignoring the dog, you will (eventually) force the behaviour into extinction. Note that the behaviour is likely to get worse before it disappears, so be sure there are not any 'softies' in the family who will give in to little 'Oliver' every time he whimpers, 'More, please.'

COPROPHAGIA

Faeces eating is, to humans, one of the most disgusting behaviours that their dogs could engage in, yet, to dogs, it is perfectly normal. It is hard for us to understand why a dog would want to eat his own faeces. He could be seeking certain nutrients that are missing from his diet, he could be just plain peckish or he could be attracted by the pleasing (to a dog) scent. While coprophagia most often refers to the dog's eating his own faeces, a dog may just as likely eat that of another animal as well if he comes across it. Dogs often find the stool of cats and

horses more palatable than that of other dogs.

Vets have found that diets with low levels of digestibility, containing relatively low levels of fibre and high levels of starch, increase coprophagia. Therefore, high-fibre diets may decrease the likelihood of dogs' eating faeces. Both the consistency of the stool (how firm it feels in the dog's mouth) and the presence of undigested nutrients increase the likelihood. Once the dog develops diarrhoea from faeces eating, he will likely stop this distasteful habit.

To discourage this behaviour, first make sure that the food you are feeding your dog is nutritionally complete and that he is getting enough food. If changes in his diet do not seem to work, and no medical cause can be found, you will have to modify the behaviour through environmental control before it becomes an habit. The best way to prevent your dog from eating his stool is to make it unavailable—clean up after he eliminates and remove any stool from the garden. If it is not there, he cannot eat it.

Reprimanding for stool eating rarely impresses the dog. Vets recommend distracting the dog while he is in the act of stool eating. Coprophagia is seen most frequently in pups 6 to 12 months of age, and usually disappears around the dog's first birthday.

Showing Your
SEALYHAM TERRIER

When you purchase your Sealyham, you will make it clear to the breeder whether you want one just as a loveable companion and pet, or if you hope to be buying a Sealyham with show prospects. No reputable breeder will sell you a young puppy and tell you that it is *definitely* of show quality, for so much can go wrong during the early months of a puppy's development. If you plan to show, what you hopefully will have acquired is a puppy with 'show potential.'

To the novice, exhibiting a Sealyham in the show ring may look easy, but it takes a lot of hard work and devotion to do top winning at a show such as the prestigious Crufts Dog Show, not to mention a little luck too!

The first concept that the canine novice learns when watching a dog show is that each dog first competes against members of its own breed. Once the judge has selected the best member of each breed (Best of Breed), provided the show is judged on a Group system, that chosen dog will compete with other dogs in its group. Finally, the best of each group will compete for Best in Show.

The second concept that you must understand is that the dogs are not actually compared against one another. The judge compares each dog against its breed standard, which is a written description of the ideal specimen of the breed. While some early breed standards were indeed based on specific dogs that were famous or popular, many dedicated enthusiasts say that a perfect specimen, as described in the standard, has never walked into a show ring, has never been bred and, to the woe of dog breeders around the globe, does not exist. Breeders attempt to get as *close* to this ideal as possible with every litter, but theoretically the 'perfect' dog is so elusive that it is impossible. (And if the 'perfect' dog were born, breeders and judges probably would never agree that it was indeed 'perfect.')

If you are interested in exploring the world of dog showing, your best bet is to join your local breed club. These clubs often host both Championship and Open Shows, and sometimes Match meetings and special events, all of which could be of interest, even if you are only an onlooker. Clubs also send out newsletters, and some organise training days and seminars in order that people may learn more about their chosen breed. To locate the breed club closest to you, contact The Kennel Club, the ruling body for the British dog world.

The Kennel Club governs not only conformation shows but also working trials, obedience shows, agility trials and field trials. The Kennel Club furnishes the rules and regulations for all of these events plus general dog registration and other basic requirements of dog ownership. Its annual show, called the Crufts Dog Show, held in Birmingham, is the largest benched show in England. Every year over 20,000 of the UK's best dogs qualify to participate in this marvellous show, which lasts four days.

The Kennel Club governs many different kinds of shows in Great Britain, Australia, South Africa and beyond. At the most competitive and prestigious of these shows, the Championship Shows, a dog can earn Challenge Certificates (CCs), and thereby become a Show Champion or a Champion. A dog must earn three CCs under three different judges to earn the prefix of 'Sh Ch' or 'Ch.' Some breeds must also qualify in a field trial in order to gain the title of full Champion,

INFORMATION ON CLUBS

You can get information about dog shows from kennel clubs and breed clubs:

Fédération Cynologique Internationale
14, rue Leopold II, B-6530 Thuin, Belgium
www.fci.be

The Kennel Club
1-5 Clarges St., Piccadilly, London W1Y 8AB
UK
www.the-kennel-club.org.uk

American Kennel Club
5580 Centerview Dr., Raleigh, NC 27606-3390
USA
www.akc.org

Canadian Kennel Club
89 Skyway Ave., Suite 100, Etobicoke, Ontario
M9W 6R4 Canada
www.ckc.ca

PRACTISE AT HOME

If you have decided to show your dog, you must train him to gait around the ring by your side at the correct pace and pattern, and to tolerate being handled and examined by the judge. Most breeds require complete dentition, all breeds require a particular bite (scissor, level or undershot) and all males must have two apparently normal testicles fully descended into the scrotum. Enlist family and friends to hold mock trials in your garden to prepare your future champion!

though the Sealyham is not one such breed. CCs are awarded to a very small percentage of the dogs competing, and dogs that are already Champions compete with others for these coveted CCs. The number of CCs awarded in any one year is based upon the total number of dogs in each breed entered for competition.

There are three types of Championship Shows: an all-breed General Championship Show for all Kennel-Club-recognised breeds; a Group Championship Show, which is limited to breeds within one of the groups; and a Breed Show, which is usually confined to a single breed. The Kennel Club determines which breeds at which Championship Shows will have the opportunity to earn CCs (or tickets). Serious exhibitors often will opt not to participate if the tickets are withheld at a particular show. This policy makes earning championships even more difficult to accomplish.

Open Shows are generally less competitive and are frequently used as 'practice shows' for young dogs. There are hundreds of Open Shows each year that can be delightful social events and are great first-show experiences for the novice. Even if you're considering just watching a show to wet your paws, an Open Show is a great choice.

While Championship and

Open Shows are the most important for the beginner to understand, there are other types of shows in which the interested dog owner can participate. Training clubs sponsor Matches that can be entered on the day of the show for a nominal fee. In these introductory-level exhibitions, two dogs' names are pulled out of an hat and 'matched,' the winner of that match goes on to the next round and eventually only one dog is left undefeated.

Exemption Shows are much more light-hearted affairs with usually only four pedigree classes and several 'fun' classes, all of which can be entered on the day of the show. Exemption Shows are sometimes held in conjunction with small agricultural shows and the proceeds must be given to a charity. Limited Shows are also available in small number. Entry is restricted to members of the club that hosts the show, although one can usually join the club when making an entry.

Before you actually step into the ring, you would be well advised to sit back and observe the judge's ring procedure. If it is your first time in the ring, do not be over-anxious and run to the front of the line. It is much better to stand back and study how the exhibitor in front of you is performing. The judge asks each handler to 'stand' the dog, hopefully showing the dog off to

HOW TO ENTER A DOG SHOW

To enter a dog show in Britain, you need to look at one of the two dog papers, which come out on Fridays and can be ordered at any newsagent. Find the phone number of the secretary of a show, and call to obtain a schedule and entry form. Fill in the form with the classes you wish to enter (double-check your form!) and do not forget to send a cheque for the entries. Show entries close six weeks or so before the date of the show.

You cannot enter the show if your dog is not registered with The Kennel Club. If you have sent off the forms to The Kennel Club to transfer the dog into your name, it is possible to enter with 'TAF' (transfer applied for) after the dog's name.

his best advantage. The judge will observe the dog from a distance and from different angles, and approach the dog to check his teeth, overall structure, alertness and muscle tone, as well as consider how well the dog 'conforms' to the standard. Most importantly, the judge will have the exhibitor move the dog around the ring in some pattern that he should specify (another advantage to not going first, but always listen since some judges change their directions—and the judge is always right!). Finally, the judge will give the dog one last look before moving on to the next exhibitor.

If you are not in the top three at your first show, do not be discouraged. Be patient and consistent, and you may eventu-

ally find yourself in the winning line-up. Remember that the winners were once in your shoes and have devoted many hours and much money to earn the placement. If you find that your dog is losing every time and never getting a nod, it may be time to consider a different dog sport or to just enjoy your Sealyham Terrier as a pet.

Virtually all countries with a recognised speciality breed club (sometimes called a 'parent' club) offer show conformation competition specifically for and among Sealyhams. Under direction of the club, other special events for going to ground, hunting, tracking, obedience and agility may be offered as well, whether for titling or just for fun.

AGILITY TRIALS

Agility trials began in the UK in 1977 and have since spread around the world, especially to the US, where they are very popular. The handler directs his dog over an obstacle course that includes jumps, as well as tyres, the dog walk, weave poles, pipe tunnels, collapsed tunnels, etc. The Kennel Club requires that dogs not be trained for agility until they are 12 months old. This dog sport is great fun for dog and owner, and interested owners should join a training club that has obstacles and experienced agility handlers who can introduce you and your dog to the 'ropes' (and tyres, tunnels, etc.).

COLOUR CONFUSION

The first-prize winner in Britain collects a red rosette and prize card. In the United States, red goes to the second-place winner, and it is the blue rosette that is awarded to the class winner. This difference in colours has led to some embarrassing situations when some have judged away from home!

CLASSES AT DOG SHOWS

There can be as many as 18 classes per sex for a breed, depending on its popularity. The classes offered can include Minor Puppy (ages 6 to 9 months), Puppy (ages 6 to 12 months), Junior (ages 6 to 18 months) and Beginners (handler or dog never won first place), as well as the following: Maiden; Novice; Tyro; Debutant; Undergraduate; Graduate; Postgraduate; Minor Limit; Mid Limit; Limit; Open; Veteran; Stud Dog; Brood Bitch; Progeny; Brace and Team. The timetable for the show, which comes with the entry form, explains each of the classes in detail.

FÉDÉRATION CYNOLOGIQUE INTERNATIONALE

Established in 1911, the Fédération Cynologique Internationale (FCI) represents the 'world kennel club.' This international body brings uniformity to the breeding, judging and showing of pure-bred dogs. Although the FCI originally included only five European nations: France, Germany, Austria, the Netherlands and Belgium (which remains its headquarters), the organisation today embraces nations on six continents and recognises well over 300 breeds of pure-bred dog.

The FCI sponsors both national and international shows. The hosting country determines the judging system and breed standards are always based on the breed's country of origin. Dogs from every country can participate in these impressive canine spectacles, the largest of which is the World Dog Show, hosted in a different country each year.

There are three titles attainable through the FCI: the International Champion, which is the most prestigious; the International Beauty Champion, which is based on aptitude

TIDINESS COUNTS

Surely you've spent hours grooming your dog to perfection for the show ring, but don't forget about yourself! While the dog should be the centre of attention, it is important that you also appear clean and tidy. Wear smart, appropriate clothes and comfortable shoes in a colour that contrasts with your dog's coat. Look and act like a professional.

SHOW RING ETIQUETTE

Just as with anything else, there is a certain etiquette to the show ring that can only be learned through experience. Showing your dog can be quite intimidating to you as a novice when it seems as if everyone else knows what he is doing. You can familiarise yourself with ring procedure beforehand by taking ringcraft classes to prepare you and your dog for conformation showing and by talking with experienced handlers. When you are in the ring, it is very important to pay attention and listen to the instructions you are given about where to move your dog. Remember, even the most skilled handlers had to start somewhere. Keep it up and you too will become a proficient handler as you gain practice and experience.

certificates in different countries; and the International Trial Champion, which is based on achievement in obedience trials in different countries. An FCI title requires a dog to win three CACs (*Certificats d'Aptitude au Championnat*), at regional or club shows under three different judges who are breed specialists. The title of International Champion is gained by winning four CACIBs (*Certificats d'Aptitude au Championnat International de Beauté*), which are offered only at international dog can be awarded a classification of Excellent, Very Good, Good, Sufficient and Not Sufficient. Puppies can be awarded classifications of Very Promising, Promising or Not Promising. Four placements are made in each class. After all classes are judged, a Best of Breed is selected. Other special groups and classes may also be shown. Each exhibitor showing a dog receives a written evaluation from the judge.

shows, with at least a one-year lapse between the first and fourth award.

The FCI is divided into ten groups. At the World Dog Show, the following classes are offered for each breed: Puppy Class (6–9 months), Junior Class (9–18 months), Open Class (15 months or older) and Champion Class. A

Besides the World Dog Show and other all-breed shows, you can exhibit your dog at speciality shows held by different breed clubs. Speciality shows may have their own regulations.

Owned by David Winsley, this history-making terrier is Ch Davmar Northern Dancer, the first Sealyham Terrier to win Best in Show at a Championship Show in the UK for over two decades, doing so in 2001. This is a superb example of the breed.

7276

INDEX

My Sealyham Terrier

PUT YOUR PUPPY'S FIRST PICTURE HERE

Dog's Name _____

Date _____ Photographer _____